The Pharmaceutical Industry

The Pharmaceutical Industry

Economics, Performance, and Government Regulation

Erol Caglarcan, Ph.D., *Hoffmann-La Roche Inc.*
Walter J. Campbell, M.B.A., *Walter Campbell Associates*
Gilbert D. Harrell, Ph.D., *Michigan State University*
Jerome E. Schnee, Ph.D., *Rutgers University*
David A. Siskind, M.I.A., *Hoffmann-La Roche Inc.*
Rodney F. Smith, Ph.D., *Clark University*

Editor:
Cotton M. Lindsay, Ph.D., *University of California, Los Angeles*

A Wiley Medical Publication
John Wiley & Sons
New York   Chichester   Brisbane   Toronto

Library of Congress Cataloging in Publication Data:

Main entry under title:

The Pharmaceutical industry.

  (A Wiley medical publication)
  Includes index.
  1. Drug trade — United States — Addresses, essays,
lectures. I. Lindsay, Cotton M. [DNLM: 1. Drug
industry. QV736 P531]

HD9666.56.P45   338.4'7'61510973   77-27062
ISBN 0-471-04077-0

Printed in the United States of America

10 9 8 7 6 5 4 3 2 1

Authors

Erol Caglarcan
Political Economist
Hoffmann-La Roche Inc.
Nutley, New Jersey

Walter J. Campbell
Walter Campbell Associates
Watertown, Massachusetts

Gilbert D. Harrell
Associate Professor of Marketing and
Transportation Administration
The Graduate School of Business
Michigan State University

Cotton M. Lindsay
Associate Professor
Department of Economics
University of California, Los Angeles

Jerome E. Schnee
Associate Professor
Graduate School of Business Administration
Rutgers University

David A. Siskind
Public Policies Analyst
Hoffmann-La Roche Inc.
Nutley, New Jersey

Rodney F. Smith
Assistant Professor
Clark University
Worcester, Massachusetts

Acknowledgments

We gratefully acknowledge the administrative and editorial assistance received from John H. Wood, Public Affairs Director of Hoffmann-La Roche Inc., who conceived the idea for this book and brought us together to work on it. In addition, we express our appreciation for Sandy Oeffler's help in coordinating and skillfully typing the final manuscript.

EROL CAGLARCAN
WALTER J. CAMPBELL
GILBERT D. HARRELL
COTTON M. LINDSAY
JEROME E. SCHNEE
DAVID A. SISKIND
RODNEY F. SMITH

Acknowledgments

Contents

Introduction
Cotton M. Lindsay

1. Governmental Control of Therapeutic Drugs:
    Intent, Impact, and Issues   9
    Jerome E. Schnee

2. Economic Structure and Performance of the
    Ethical Pharmaceutical Industry   23
    Jerome E. Schnee
    Erol Caglarcan

3. Contributions of the Pharmaceutical Industry to
    Improved Health   41
    David A. Siskind

4. Pharmaceutical Marketing   69
    Gilbert D. Harrell

5. The Changing Pharmaceutical Research and
    Development Environment   91
    Jerome E. Schnee
    Erol Caglarcan

6. Profitability and the Pharmaceutical Industry   105
    Walter J. Campbell
    Rodney F. Smith

7. The Emerging Health Care Environment: Selected Issues   119
    Walter J. Campbell

    Conclusion   141
    Cotton M. Lindsay

    Index   149

The Pharmaceutical Industry

Introduction

Cotton M. Lindsay
Associate Professor
Department of Economics
University of California, Los Angeles

Dispassionate discussion of the economics of the pharmaceutical industry is rare. Drugs offer a cure for the sick, relief to those in pain, a measure of tranquility to the anxious and depressed, and occasionally life to those at death's door. We quite naturally react with a certain abhorrence to the idea that people in need of drugs for one of these reasons are required to pay for them at all. The suggestion that the prices paid may be held artificially high through collusion or through restrictive patent arrangements stirs not only our intellectual interest but our indignation.

Yet we must attempt to suppress this visceral reaction and give the issues careful attention, for the stakes are high. Impulsive errors here may produce more than mere reductions in national income. They may cause unnecessary misery and needless loss of life. It is tempting to yield to the vacuous sloganeering on both sides of the debate over the future of medicine and pharmaceuticals in this country. From one side, we are asked to reject government involvement in medicine solely because it is *government* involvement, reflecting an unwillingness to analyze realistically the need for or the results of that presence. From the other side, we are exhorted to commit through the public sector indefinitely large amounts of resources to the task of keeping people healthy—without inquiring whether such a commitment is likely to improve health and life in general or at what cost.

In this volume the reader will find little to support either of these two extreme positions. One can find here, however, a valuable introduction to the factual background before which the rhetorical battle rages. Each chapter seeks to present an objective and impartial survey of the scientific literature bearing on a different aspect of the pharmaceutical industry. The topics considered range from the economic performance of firms in the industry to the performance of the industry in producing new therapeutic agents. Discussion extends from marketing practices of pharmaceutical companies to an appraisal of the changing economics of the health care environment in which this industry plays such an important role.

Together the discussions present a broad and provocative tableau of issues and evidence, of aspirations by lawmakers, and the results of programs born of those hopes. The policymaker intent on informing himself on these issues will not want to stop with this book, but he will find here a helpful guide to the factual core of much of the controversy. And though, as of this writing, many of the issues remain unresolved, these papers will guide the concerned reader toward evidence he should seek from forthcoming research.

This book is not intended to present solutions, nor to provide a basis for legislation. Hopefully, its principal effect will be to demonstrate the number of important unanswered questions which should be addressed before additional legislative "solutions" to any perceived problems are sought. If the cost of greater safety or lower drug prices is a reduction in the rate of development, there is need for more precise numerical estimates of this cost. If greater safety has been purchased by increasing the cost of such development, we should try to establish how much more costly research has been made *and* how much safety we are actually provided through these extensive premarketing control programs.

We have not been poorly served by the pharmaceutical industry during the century of its existence — even during the lengthy period when little regulation or supervision by government was practiced. The industry has provided us with a host of drugs which have revolutionized the practice of medicine, and it has provided them at prices that have steadily declined relative to the consumer price index. Although profits have been substantial, for the most part they have been reinvested in research and development, making possible a future even freer of disease than the present. Legislation and regulation in this area must proceed with an eye ever-fixed on the potential impact of new policy on that future as well.

Policies that attack prices and profits directly through regulation, controls, or weakened patents will also lead to reduced research and development effort. The advisability of such policies must be considered after a frank appraisal of the magnitude of their potential costs as well as their benefits. The benefits are immediate and visible. The costs seem more remote and conjectural. The benefits of a price rollback are apparent to everyone, as are the advantages of strict monitoring of drug safety. When a drug is found to have unknown side effects — perhaps fatal side effects — the victims are specific people. They have names, faces, families, and friends. Their situation is depicted in vivid detail on front pages and network news.

Policies promoting price controls and ever-stricter policing of drugs are not without their own hapless victims, however. The plight of these victims is less newsworthy. Therefore, we are less conscious of the real costs they bear. This remoteness from the public consciousness does not diminish the cost, however. Today, there are roughly 5 million Americans with heart disease. Another 3 million have cancer, and 600,000 more will develop some form of the disease within a year. Many others will contract other diseases for which we presently have no cure. Every policy that inhibits investment in pharmaceutical research delays the introduction of medicines which might eventually save lives and reduce human suffering. The fact that 2000 Americans die daily of heart disease does not make the front page very often, but in a real sense these individuals, too, are victims of public policy. The chapters in this volume help to bring into focus the real issues at stake here.

In the first chapter, Schnee discusses governmental control of drugs and its impact on the drug industry. He notes that the increased activism of government, emerging out of the 1962 amendments to the Food, Drug and Cosmetic Act, has accomplished three things:

1. Certain drugs that were found to be ineffective have been eliminated.
2. We now have assurance that each new drug has undergone thorough testing before it is marketed.
3. Claims for drugs are now closely monitored, and evidence supporting these claims must be accumulated to substantiate their validity before they are made.

These accomplishments have not been costless, however. Also attributable to this activism are three negative effects. First, there has been a sharp reduction in the number of new chemical entities developed by pharmaceutical companies as well as a lag in the introduction of new drugs in the United States compared to other countries. Second, these efforts have raised the cost of pharmaceutical research and development. Consequently, competition in the industry has been diminished because small companies now experience difficulty in financing the large outlays required to bring a new product to market.

Finally, the FDA, in its intervention into the drug market, has undeniably usurped a part of the role of the prescribing physician. There is much more at stake here than a mere jurisdictional dispute. It is far from obvious that government agencies subject to the political vicissitudes and pressures natural to such an environment can make better decisions about suitable drugs than our own physicians can make. Schnee raises some provocative questions bearing on this issue.

Drugs have different therapeutic value and other effects on different people. Our personal physicians can be aware of different properties of different drugs and our own sensitivities to these chemicals in ways that no government agency or central procurement bureau can possibly be. Individual reactions to "chemically equivalent" drugs have been shown to vary to a far greater degree than one might be led to suspect on the basis of such FDA-sanctioned "equivalency." In considering the desirability of such a usurpation of the physician's traditional role, we must therefore consider, in addition to increase in safety and the lower price that might result, the loss of the potential advantages which more independence on the part of physicians might provide.

Another issue raised by Schnee concerns the timing of testing. The FDA now relies almost exclusively on testing prior to marketing with few resources devoted to gathering information on drugs already approved for distribution. Serious doubts have been raised concerning the appropriateness of this division of resources between premarketing and postmarketing control. Most FDA-mandated testing involves the use of animals whose reactions are imperfectly correlated with effects of drugs in humans.

Second, the practice of premarketing control assumes that drug toxicity can be reliably detected at this early stage of development. Yet, evidence on this is weak. Serious side effects occur so infrequently that they are usually not identified during the premarketing testing period. The only way to accumulate information on the effects of such drugs is to market them under carefully monitored conditions. Admittedly, such a policy runs the risk of exposing the recipients to potential harmful effects of drugs. Advocates of postmarketing control argue that the present program is not entirely free of this exposure either.

In Chapter 2 Schnee and Caglarcan present a helpful overview of the development of the ethical drug industry from its crude beginnings a century ago to its critical importance today as the right arm of the modern physician. Most of their attention is focused on the current market structure of the industry, however. Their findings lend support to the view that profits and research are related. The picture that emerges is one of an industry characterized by vigorous competition at several levels. Data on entry into various therapeutic markets, market share instability, and individual price flexibility suggest that conventional market rivalry here operates to a surprising degree to hold costs and prices down. It is the introduction of successful new products that causes the high rate of turnover among pharmaceutical firms. Of the twenty major industries analyzed, the drug industry has the second highest index of market share instability.

The wide attention paid to charitable, foundation, and government-sponsored medical research may lead one to suspect that diminished interest by pharmaceutical companies in research might easily be compensated for by expanding efforts through these other channels. While this alternative exists in principle, a careful reading of Siskind's essay on the contributions of pharmaceutical firms to modern medicine raises reservations about this potential. Of all new chemical entities introduced, seven out of eight were by pharmaceutical research laboratories. Among these number most sulfonamides, mass-produced penicillin, streptomycin, and tetracycline. This is not to argue that the contributions of the public and voluntary sectors are negligible. On the contrary, important discoveries have originated in these environments as well. The fact remains, however, that most of the pharmaceutical products prescribed today were developed by the industry. It is a sobering thought to reflect where medicine would be now had policies inimical to drug industry research been adopted thirty or forty years ago.

Harrell's paper on pharmaceutical marketing reveals a seldom-recognized secondary role played by pharmaceutical firms. Marketing information provided by these firms is relied upon heavily by physicians as a source of data on new developments. More than half of the physicians contacted in a survey discussed in this essay reported that they were influenced in their prescribing decisions by information provided by industry sales representatives. Only one fourth reported that they were influenced by research reported in professional journals. The Food and Drug Administration monitors the factual content of marketing messages and mandates the inclusion of information on potential hazards of drugs. Advertising, whose role in the "affluent society" has been the object of much derisive comment since World War II, is shown here to perform an undeniably important function.

In Chapter 5, Schnee and Caglarcan survey the changing environment in which research and development take place in the pharmaceutical industry. On the one hand, the cost of research has risen dramatically. It is estimated that the cost of bringing a new pharmaceutical product to market is now more than ten times greater than it was before 1962. At least a significant part of this increase in cost is the result of the additional testing required by the 1962 amendments to the Food, Drug, and Cosmetic Act. On the other hand, research itself is becoming intrinsically less attractive for investment as the likelihood of new discoveries diminishes. Many of the drugs developed during the 1950s and early 1960s resulted from the great strides made in the biological sciences during those years. Scientific advance in biology in recent years has not been accompanied by a similar bounty of applied knowledge.

Both effects have combined to reduce significantly the output of new drugs. The rate of introduction of new products has declined to one-half its peak reached in the late 1950s. This is also reflected in the diminished rate of return earned on investment in research and development, from 11.4 percent in 1960 to 3.3 percent in 1974.

No direct measures of the sensitivity of new drug development to reductions of profitability associated with price or profit controls have been estimated or reported here, but Schnee and Caglarcan present considerable indirect evidence that investment in research and research results are both affected by the expected profitability of this activity. The slower technological process of discovery and stricter regulation of the testing phase of new drug development have led jointly to an increase in the costlines of research and development and a corresponding decrease in the profitability of such activity. Schnee and Caglarcan report that, associated with the diminished economic rewards of this activity, there has been a decline in the development of basic new pharmaceutical agents from over 30 per year in the 1950s, to 20 per year in the early 1960s, to 12 per year in the late 1960s.

Attention is also focused on the effect of the Kefauver-Harris Act on the rate of innovation. The Schnee and Caglarcan survey suggests that the amendments alone are responsible for a 50 percent decline in the rate of introduction of new chemical entities. The result is a significant "drug lag" concerning not only usage but medical awareness of new drugs between America and European countries. This effect of strict testing standards applied to new drug developments has been estimated to produce a significant social net loss of economic welfare when the benefits of stricter testing are allowed for.

In their study of drug industry profitability, Campbell and Smith note that the rate of return earned here is higher than that earned on average for all manufacturing. In this connection, however, it should also be noted that the research and development intensity in pharmaceuticals has been well over twice as high as the mean for all manufacturing industries for at least the decade reported there. However, high rates of return to capital invested in the pharmaceutical industry have persisted, giving rise to some speculation that unwarranted barriers to entry may exist in the drug industry. In view of the high turnover rate among firms here, however, it is difficult to deny the extent of competition and freedom of entry in the industry. Explanations advanced for at least part of this persistent high rate of return are, first, the growth in demand for pharmaceuticals, second, accounting treatment of research and development investment in calculating these profit rates and finally, the riskiness of investment in this area. Although these explanations do not completely account for the high rates of return, they do reduce the unexplained margin considerably. On the subject of profits, Harrell also points out that net earnings (including corporate profit tax) as a percentage of retail sales are only 11 percent. Price or profit controls which *completely eliminated profits and the profits tax* would therefore lead on average to a one-time rollback of prices equivalent to less than two years' increase in the consumer price index. A reduction in profits which merely reduced the rate of return to "normal" levels would have an almost imperceptible effect on retail prices.

In Chapter 7, Campbell sketches a possible future for the medical-care industry in the United States. He foresees slower growth here as the expansionary pressures initiated with the adoption of Medicare and Medicaid are finally accommodated. The rapid growth in hospitalizatin will also diminish — not only as new government-financed demands are satisfied — but because of changing demographic patterns, changing attitudes regarding the efficacy of medical care in "solving" health problems, and institutional changes such as the creation of professional standards review organizations and utilization review committees.

He points out further the dangers which these developments may hold for the industry. As government involvement in the industry grows, the pressure for adoption of generic drug substitution will also grow. As a result, the profit level of the industry is likely to decline. There are two reasons for this outcome. First, generic drug substitution, government-negotiated prices, and similar practices are lowering revenues of pharmaceutical companies. Second, research costs have increased dramatically.

1

Governmental Control of Therapeutic Drugs: Intent, Impact, and Issues

Jerome E. Schnee

Associate Professor
Graduate School of Business Administration
Rutgers University

HISTORY

Governmental control of drugs dates back to the 1906 Pure Food and Drugs Act. Since the principal objective of the 1906 act was to prevent and control food adulteration and abuse, drug regulation was of secondary importance. Between 1906 and 1938—when a new Food, Drug, and Cosmetic Act was signed—drug regulators concentrated on protecting the public against medical quacks and prohibiting the sale of dangerous drugs.[1]

The passage of the 1938 act signaled a shift in the intent of drug regulation. The elixir sulfanilamide tragedy of 1937 revealed the risks associated with new drugs and pointed up the need to test them for safety.[2] Before the mid-1930s, few drugs had been introduced and, consequently, problems of new drug regulation attracted little attention.

Procedures for the premarketing clearance of new drugs were among the most important provisions of the 1938 legislation. The regulations were designed to protect the public from untested and potentially harmful drugs.

[1]For more detailed historical accounts, see Cornelius C. Regier, "The Struggle for Federal Food and Drugs Legislation," *Law and Contemporary Problems* (December, 1933), pp. 3-4; and John B. Blake, ed., *Safeguarding the Public: Historical Aspects of Medicinal Drug Control* (Baltimore and London: The Johns Hopkins Press, 1970).

[2]Harry F. Dowling, *Medicines for Man* (New York: Alfred A. Knopf, 1970), p.193.

In practice, the institution of premarketing safety tests was more the result of self-regulation by pharmaceutical manufacturers than of direct government control. Pharmaceutical companies initiated such testing programs because the elixir sulfanilamide experience of 1937 had made them keenly aware of the legal liability associated with the marketing of unsafe drugs. It was not until 1963 that the federal government directly exerted control over a company's investigational plans prior to submission of a new drug application.

While the 1938 act was generally regarded as strong legislation, several drug industry practices remained unregulated. One controversial aspect of industry performance was the process used to select drugs for clinical trial. Since there was no regulation of clinical drug research before marketing, the industry could unilaterally decide whether and in what manner to test new drugs. While extensive pharmacological and toxicological data were generated for some compounds, other drugs received a minimal preclinical workup. The problems of limited toxicity testing could be compounded by human trials which, by today's standards, sometimes were poorly designed and/or executed.

The legal powers of the Food and Drug Administration on these issues were somewhat ambiguous between 1938 and 1962. The 1938 act empowered the FDA to concern itself with the safety of a product but not specifically with its efficacy. Thus, the law's language permitted the FDA to approve a drug that might be ineffective provided it was safe. To the extent that decisions about safety involved consideration of the specific ways in which a drug was to be used, efficacy was indirectly evaluated before 1962.

The most significant characteristic of the pre-1962 FDA approach is that the agency did not enter the picture until a manufacturer sought approval for marketing. It was the responsibility of each drug firm, in conjunction with individual clinical investigators, to determine the extent of clinical research that was to be performed with a new drug. Drug firms were also responsible for determining the scope and detail of the postmarketing toxicity data that were furnished to the FDA.

THE 1962 AMENDMENTS

The impetus for changing the 1938 law came from hearings begun in 1959 by Senator Estes Kefauver's Antitrust and Monopoly Subcommittee. These hearings were prompted by a belief that the prevailing federal regulations permitted the introduction of new drugs of questionable efficacy that were sold at high prices. Senator Kefauver attempted to show that nonefficacious drugs and high prices were the result of a combination of patent protection for new chemical entities, consumer and physician ignorance, and minimal incentive for physicians to consider patient drug costs.[3]

Senator Kefauver concluded that accurate information about new drugs would be provided only if the government regulated manufacturers' claims of effectiveness. A proposal to institute such regulation was included in a bill he sponsored in 1961, and a modification was incorporated in the 1962 amendments.

Some observers claim that the 1962 amendments would not have been enacted without the thalidomide episode of 1962-1963. Although the FDA used the provisions of the 1938 law to keep thalidomide from the American market, the drug had been distributed to some physicians for experimental purposes. Under the provisions of the 1938 act, the manufacturer was permitted to distribute a drug to qualified experts as long as the drug bore a label warning the expert that it was still under investigation. The American manufacturer of thalidomide ended investigational distribution of the drug and withdrew its new drug application (NDA) after reports that deformed babies had been born to European mothers who had used the drug during pregnancy. These reports aroused additional concern in the United States that clinical testing of new drugs was insufficiently regulated.[4]

The 1962 amendments to the 1938 Food, Drug, and Cosmetic Act and the subsequent implementing regulations reflected both the concerns raised in the Kefauver hearings and those arising from the thalidomide episode. The amendments had two major objectives: (1) closer control over the premarket testing of new drugs; and (2) altering the criteria for the approval to market new drugs.

With respect to drug testing, the amendments and implementing regulations empowered the FDA to specify the testing procedure a manufacturer must use to produce acceptable information for evaluating the NDA. The sponsor of a new drug was required to submit a "Notice of Claimed Investigatinal Exemption for a New Drug" to the FDA prior to human testing. The investigational new drug (IND) form is actually required to permit the interstate shipment of new drugs for clinical studies. The major impact of the IND was to require comprehensive data on animal tests before the FDA would

---

[3]The details of the Kefauver hearings are contained in U.S., Congress, Senate, Judiciary Committee, *Administered Prices: Drugs* (Washington, D.C.: Government Printing Office, 1961), especially Chapters 6-15. A more popularized version of the Kefauver hearings and the subsequent congressional debate leading to the 1962 amendments may be found in Richard Harris, *The Real Voice* (New York: Macmillan, 1964).

[4]Harris, *loc. cit.*

allow human trials. Subsequently, animal toxicologists at the FDA formulated minimum standards for a satisfactory animal testing program.[5]

With respect to drug introductions, the amendments added a proof-of-efficacy requirement to the proof-of-safety requirement of the 1938 law. No new drug may now be marketed unless and until the FDA determines not only that the drug is safe, as required under the 1938 law, but also that there is "substantial evidence," according to statutory scientific criteria, that it is effective for its intended use. An effective drug, in this context, is one which the FDA determines, on the basis of adequate clinical studies, will meet the claims made for it by the manufacturer. Further, promotion of all prescription drugs can claim no more than the effects established before the FDA and must include a summary of the side effects, contraindications, and effectiveness.

The amendments also removed the time constraint on the FDA's disposition of a new drug application. Previously, an NDA was automatically approved by the FDA if the agency failed to respond within a period of 60 days. The 1962 guidelines provided the FDA with six months to review an application and the authority to renew the six-month review period without limit.

THE IMPACT OF THE 1962 AMENDMENTS

The impact of the 1962 amendments and subsequent FDA implementing regulations remains an open and controversial issue. Although the full effects of the 1962 legislation are not completely resolved, a more complete picture of positive and negative consequences has begun to emerge.[6]

On the positive side, three major accomplishments may be identified. First, ineffective new drugs no longer reach the marketplace, since all new drugs introduced since 1962 are required to have proof of efficacy. Also, through a comprehensive scientific review involving the National Academy of Sciences/National Research Council, the FDA has arranged for the examination of drugs introduced prior to 1962 and has moved to withdraw ineffective

[5]E.I. Goldenthal, "Current Views on Safety Evaluation of Drugs," *Food and Drug Administration Papers* (May, 1968), p.13.

[6]The economic impacts of the 1962 legislation are discussed in Sam Peltzman, *Regulation of Pharmaceutical Innovation: The 1962 Amendments* (Washington, D.C.: American Enterprise Institute, 1974). The impacts of governmental practice on the drug development process and on the conduct of medical practice are discussed in William M. Wardell and Louis Lasagna, *Regulation and Drug Development* (Washington, D.C.: American Enterprise Institute, 1975). The Wardell and Lasagna volume is the most up-to-date, comprehensive account of how governmental regulation has influenced the drug development process. Many of the ideas discussed in subsequent sections of this chapter are based on the more comprehensive discussion in that book.

drugs from the market. Second, untested new medicines are a thing of the past. New drugs must pass comprehensive and rigorous animal tests before human testing may begin. Then, extensive clinical trials are mandatory before marketing clearance will be granted by the FDA. Third, since 1962, there has been control over the accuracy of claims for prescription drugs and communication of their features, benefits, and risks.

On the negative side, three dysfunctional, and largely unanticipated, consequences of the 1962 legislation have developed. First, there has been a sharp reduction in the number of new chemical entities introduced in the United States since 1962. That is, while the 1962 amendments have ensured that the available drugs are, on average, more effective, they have also contributed to a reduction in the number of effective drugs introduced to the market. As a result, the United States has lagged behind other countries in the introduction of new drugs.[7]

A second negative impact of the 1962 amendments is their effect on competition in the U.S. pharmaceutical industry. Enforcement of the 1962 amendments seems to have entrenched the positions of the larger firms and resulted in increased concentration.[8] One reason for the increasing dominance of large firms is that there are fewer new, effective drugs appearing to challenge the market positions of older drugs. In addition, the dramatic increases in the costs of drug development have made it increasingly difficult for smaller firms to develop and introduce new products.[9]

A third, unanticipated consequence of tighter drug regulation is that government has become an active partner in the practice of medicine. In passing judgment on the safety and efficacy of medicines, committees of experts commissioned by the FDA now hold recommendatory powers over matters that were formerly regarded as the province of the physician and the patient. Drug promotion and other communications to physicians are restricted to a set of approved uses for a given drug. Physicians also have been denied access to particular drugs. Many members of the medical community consider this participation of the federal government and expert advisory committees in matters of medical practice a serious intrusion into the physician-

[7]William M. Wardell, "Introduction of New Therapeutic Drugs in the United States and Great Britain: An International Comparison," *Clinical Pharmacology and Therapeutics*, Vol. 14 (1973), pp. 773-90.

[8]Peltzman, *op. cit.*, Chapter VI; Henry G. Grabowski, John M. Vernon, and Lacy Glenn Thomas, "The Effects of Regulatory Policy on The Incentives to Innovate: An International Comparative Analysis," *Impact of Public Policy on Drug Innovation and Pricing*, eds. Samuel A. Mitchell and Emery A. Link (Washington, D.C.: The American University, 1976).

[9]Harold Clymer, "The Changing Costs and Risks of Pharmaceutical Innovation," *The Economics of Drug Innovation*, ed. Joseph D. Cooper (Washington, D.C.: The American University, 1970), pp.115-116.

patient relationship and a potentially harmful consequence of drug regulation.

THE PHILOSOPHY OF DRUG REGULATION

Given the substantial controversy that surrounds current drug regulatory practices, it is useful to question whether the 1962 amendments, in principle and intent, meet the needs of the public. In order to address this issue, it is necessary to define the needs of the public with respect to drug therapy.

Essentially, the public requires that drugs, which are highly effective for specific illnesses when used appropriately by physicians, be available. Such drugs should carry an acceptable degree of risk for the likely benefit to be obtained. These drugs should be readily available, and their prices should be competitive and bear some relationship to the benefits they provide. Over the longer term, the public's requirements extend to the continuing development of safer and more effective ways of using all therapies.

Patients delegate the choice of drug decision to physicians. Therefore, the public's needs must be defined in terms of physicians' requirements for effective drug therapy. From the standpoint of physicians, third-party assistance is needed to: (1) ensure the quality of drugs; (2) ensure bioavailability and drug equivalence; and (3) disseminate efficacy and toxicity data.[10] Federal controls to ensure that a drug is of defined chemical compositon, high quality, and correct weight or potency date back to the 1906 Pure Food and Drugs Act. Bioavailability refers to the rate and extent of absorption of the administered drug in the blood stream. Drug equivalence relates to the therapeutic similarity of different forms of the same drug. Since the 1930s, bioavailability controls have been designed in an attempt to ensure that all dosage forms of a particular drug are safe and appropriate for the intended use.

The regulation of therapeutic equivalence has become extremely controversial due to the increased importance of generic drugs. Many generic drugs are available at lower prices than corresponding brand-name drugs. Because the generic drugs are usually not subject to the same extensive clinical testing, there is often considerable concern that they may not produce a corresponding equivalent therapeutic effect in patients. In fact, certain generic drugs have been shown to be therapeutically inequivalent to the branded formulation.

As yet, the scientific and regulatory question of how close the generic product should be to the original, clinically tested product remains unresolved. Answers to these questions require further advances in the science of clinical

---

[10]Wardell and Lasagna, *op. cit.*, pp. 130-131.

pharmacology. Some observers have concluded that to protect a patient from the risk of potentially inferior medicines, therapeutic equivalence cannot be assumed but must be demonstrated on the basis of sound scientific evidence. Some have also concluded that, in light of the state of the scientific art, it is too early to impose rigid controls over required therapeutic equivalence for generic products.

The collection and dissemination of efficacy and toxicity data should preferably be performed on a national scale. There is debate, however, concerning the current methods used by private firms and the government to compile and disseminate efficacy and safety data and the need for direct federal participation. Those who question the need for governmental control of information collection and dissemination contend that the American Medical Association was actively involved in this effort long before the federal government undertook this responsibility. The government's efforts essentially focus on legal requirements, whereas the AMA's *Drug Evaluations* and the drug evaluations performed by independent publications, such as *The Medical Letter*, seek to communicate meaningful information to the physician.[11]

Federal control over the dissemination of information covers both drug labeling and advertising and centers on the package insert, which appears in each package shipped by the drug manufacturer. The package insert is both a medical and legal document and contains current medical knowledge concerning safety and effectiveness of a drug. One principal drawback has been the lack of incidence figures on adverse reactions; however, the FDA recently proposed new regulations that require the inclusion of such data in the package insert.

OPERATIONAL ISSUES IN DRUG REGULATION

Critics of the current U.S. system for regulating drugs emphasize the distinction between legislative provisions and the interpretation and implementation of these provisions by the FDA. There appears to be general agreement that the premarketing safety tests required by the 1938 act and the 1962 amendments, covering investigational plans, proof of efficacy, and control over certain aspects of advertising, are consistent with the needs of patients. The difficulty is the widening gap between legislative intent and principle, on the one hand, and regulatory practice, on the other.

[11]American Medical Association, *AMA Drug Evaluations* (Chicago: American Medical Association, 1971); and The Medical Letter, Inc., *The Medical Letter* (New Rochelle, New York).

One such problem is that the terms "safety" and "efficacy" do not have operational meanings suitable for the present state-of-the-art in the science of drug evaluation. There is substantial disagreement between pharmaceutical firms and the FDA as to the scope and extent of the data needed to demonstrate evidence of safety and efficacy. The debate extends to whether currently available data satisfy perceived requirements, whether a particular degree of safety or efficacy is sufficient for the intended use, and what uses should be deemed appropriate.

The wording of the present law recognizes the current limitations of clinical pharmacology. However, the rigid, legalistic interpretation of the law exceeds the scientific limitations in drug evaluation. Current inadequacies include an inability to evaluate multiple drug effects, a disregard of the total therapeutic situation, and difficulty balancing diverse beneficial effects against diverse toxic effects.[12]

A second difficulty is that current regulatory practice does not distinguish between the need to determine appropriate uses of a drug for the population, as a whole, and the need for physicians to determine appropriate uses in individual patients. Because the therapeutic effect of a specific drug on a given patient must be observed empirically, individual physicians may have a comparative advantage over expert committees in deciding the appropriate uses of drugs. The experience of other countries[13] and the reaction of the American medical community suggest that the approval of some uses and disapproval of others on a community-wide basis is not in the best interests of all patients.[14]

A third operational issue concerns the selection of control points in the regulatory evaluation of drugs. Government controls in this country are almost completely based on premarketing, as opposed to postmarketing, evaluation. Control is exercised over both preclinical (animal) and clinical evaluations. The major difficulty in regulatory evaluation of animal test data is that, frequently, there is limited correlation between the results of animal tests and subsequent clinical test finding. The action of some drugs, such as acetylsalicylic acid and phenylbutazone, is demonstrable only in man. For agents of this type, animal tests are of little predictive value.[15]

[12]A. Feinstein, "How Do We Measure 'Safety' and 'Efficacy'?," Lancet, Vol. 2 (1972), pp. 554-58.

[13]William M. Wardell, "Control of Drug Utilization in the Context of a National Health Service: The New Zealand System," Clinical Pharmacology and Therapeutics, Vol. 16 (1974), pp. 585-94.

[14]Wardell and Lasagna, op. cit., p. 137.

[15]John T. Litchfield, "Forecasting Drug Effects in Man from Studies in Laboratory Animals," Journal of the American Medical Association, Vol. 177, No. 34 (July, 1961).

Because of these technical barriers, caution must be exercised that animal testing requirements are not excessively stringent. Current FDA animal testing requirements probably exceed those necessary to protect the humans involved in the earliest clinical studies. If this is so, potentially valuable drugs are being unjustifiably discarded because of overly restrictive animal testing requirements. The comments of Wardell and Lasagna are instructive:

> If even one new drug of the stature of penicillin or digitalis has been unjustifiably banished to a company's back shelf because of excessively stringent animal requirements, that event will have harmed more people than have been affected by all the toxicity that has occurred in the history of modern drug development. It is entirely conceivable that the losses from excessively conservative interpretation of animal toxicity tests are more harmful than the toxicity that would be experienced if drugs were tested in man, with appropriate safeguards, at an earlier stage.[16]

There is no way to know how many valuable pharmaceuticals may have been discarded in this way. Furthermore, there are presently insufficient safeguards in the drug development process to prevent the loss of useful drugs.

A related aspect of the drug testing issue is the emphasis placed on premarketing clinical trials. The current regulatory approach assumes that important side effects in man can reliably be detected at an early stage of clinical investigation. Clinical pharmacologists have raised serious questions about the validity of this assumption. They note that only a limited number of patients can be studied intensively during clinical trials. As a result, the only side effects that can be detected at all in the premarketing stage are those that occur relatively frequently.[17]

The significant point is that premarketing studies of any realistic size have very little chance of detecting rare but important side effects. It is these rare side effects that lead to widespread, and sometimes catastrophic, drug toxicity after a product is marketed. One study has, in fact, documented that widespread drug toxicity only occurs after a drug has been marketed, and never in the early phases of development. This finding implies that premarketing observations can never be an adequate substitute for effective postmarketing surveillance.[18]

Nevertheless, drug regulation in the United States has relied almost completely on control over preclinical and premarketing testing with limited attention given to postmarketing surveillance. The United States reporting rate

---

[16]Wardell and Lasagna, *op. cit.*, p. 138.

[17]*Ibid.*, p. 139.

[18]J. Barnes and F. Denz, "Experimental Methods Used in Determining Chronic Toxicity," *Pharmacology Review*, Vol. 6 (1954), p. 191.

is among the lowest of all twelve countries reporting to the World Health Organization International Drug Monitoring Program.[19] Moreover, American physicians received no meaningful feedback from the U.S. monitoring system until 1974. The FDA's adverse reaction reporting system, which is another element in this country's postmarketing surveillance, was criticized in a 1974 U.S. General Accounting Office report.[20]

PROPOSALS FOR MODIFYING DRUG REGULATION

Several recommendations have been advanced to create a regulatory system which is more conducive to the discovery and development of new drugs, on the one hand, and the effective utilization of drugs, on the other. These suggestions center on the need for: (a) more realistic premarketing requirements; (b) more effective postmarketing surveillance; and (c) more effective control over the utilization of drugs by physicians.

The major criticism of present FDA controls over drug development is that a drug's potential hazards receive more emphasis than the drug's potential benefits. Wardell's study of the drug lag makes it clear that the marketing of new, valuable drugs in the United States has been delayed or abandoned because of this unbalanced emphasis of federal regulators.[21]

The current FDA approach presumes that the earliest clinical studies are the most hazardous phase of clinical investigation. However, the available evidence suggests that these initial human studies are the safest of clinical investigations. This is due, in part, to the fact that the subjects in these studies are the most carefully monitored. Moreover, as previously stated, widespread toxicity does not occur in the early stages of a drug's development. Consequently, it has been suggested that the preclinical stage of drug development be compressed by releasing compounds much earlier for clinical investigation.[22]

Another aspect of establishing more realistic premarketing requirements is the need to distinguish between the therapeutic and investigational use of unmarketed drugs. Because of the lengthy new drug approval process in this country, there are always unmarketed products which would benefit some pa-

[19]World Health Organization, "Research Project for International Drug Monitoring," Report No. 3 (1972).

[20]U.S., Comptroller General, *A Report to the Congress: Assessment of the Food and Drug Administration's Handling of Reports on Adverse Reactions from the Use of Drugs* (Washington, D.C.: U.S. General Accounting Office, 1974).

[21]Wardell, "Introduction of New Therapeutic Drugs," *op. cit*, pp. 773-90.

[22]Source data on this subject are reviewed in Wardell and Lasagna, *op. cit.*, p. 146.

tients. In the present system, a new, useful drug cannot be promoted until the FDA approves it. Until then, doctors may not even be aware of it. Even when the patient or his doctor is aware of the existence of an unmarketed drug and the patient genuinely needs it, he has no guaranteed access to the product in this country. There is a need to modify the cumbersome process so that investigational drugs are available to patients who really need them.

The existence of a successful postmarketing surveillance program could permit the more rapid marketing of new drugs while not exposing the public to any additional harm. Two sets of proposals have been advanced to overcome the inadequacies of the current U.S. system. Under one approach, drugs such as Depo-Provera, levodopa, and methadone for maintenance programs have been released under monitored or restricted conditions in the United States.[23]

Recently, Senators Kennedy and Javits introduced new legislation that would amend the Federal Food, Drug, and Cosmetic Act to revise the current, all-or-nothing method of drug approval. The proposed legislation adds a fourth phase to the current three-phase system for clinically investigating drugs. This fourth phase, Phase D, would make it possible to introduce a new drug into drug distribution channels on a limited basis without full NDA approval. In addition to the determination of safety and effectiveness, this new phase would also be concerned with unanticipated, potential new uses; patterns of use; and other factors necessary for establishing drug profiles.[24]

Response to the proposed legislation has been mixed. For example, representatives of the pharmaceutical industry contend that Phase D is likely to make the drug approval process too lengthy and costly unless some of the requirements of Phases A, B, and C are relaxed. There is also concern that the proposed amendment provides the FDA commissioner too much discretion in deciding whether or not a new drug should pass through a controlled distribution and reporting stage.

A second aspect of an effective surveillance program would involve increased utilization of foreign data on drug efficacy and toxicity. Until recently, official FDA policy with respect to overseas experience was very parochial.

[23]A review of the National Cancer Institute's experience with the therapeutic use of investigational drugs and general suggestions for improvement are both contained in C. G. Zubrod, "Development and Marketing of Prescription Drugs," U.S., Senate, Committee on Small Business, *Hearings on Competitive Problems in the Drug Industry*, Part 23, 93rd Cong., 1st Sess., 1973, pp. 9672-88.

[24]U.S., Congress, Senate, S. 1831, *Bill to Amend the Public Health Services Act; and to Amend the Federal Food, Drug, and Cosmetic Act*, 95th Cong., 1st Sess., July 11, 1977; and U.S., Congress, Senate, S. 2040, *Bill to Amend the Federal Food, Drug, and Cosmetic Act*, 95th Cong., 1st Sess., August 5, 1977.

Wardell and Lasagna claim that "in some therapeutic areas FDA policy was to regard all evidence of harm from abroad as acceptable no matter how poor its quality, while no evidence of efficacy or benefit was acceptable no matter how high its quality."[25]

The FDA does acknowledge that its review of a new drug application has relied almost exclusively on clinical investigations performed in the United States. The FDA's acknowledgement of data generated from clinical studies in other countries was primarily limited to reviews of published literature. In April 1975, the FDA altered its policy to permit the submission of efficacy data obtained outside the United States.[26] While progress has thus been made to utilize foreign data as supportive evidence in the new drug approval process, greater efforts are required to incorportate foreign data into a comprehensive postmarketing surveillance program.

The present drug regulatory system centers on the control of new product marketing. Critics contend that such marketing controls do not guarantee proper therapeutic use of a drug. One proposal to improve drug utilization was issued by Senator Kennedy during his March 1976 address to the annual meeting of the Pharmaceutical Manufacturers Association. Senator Kennedy called on the pharmaceutical industry to create and fund an independent, nonprofit corporation to oversee the collection of adequate drug use data. This proposal was based on the Senate Health Subcommittee's finding that there is no accurate evidence concerning actual drug usage by the average American physician.[27] The creation of the Joint Commission on Prescription Drug Use was the first step in an industry-supported attempt to remedy this situation. The commission, which held its first meeting in November 1976, will design a postmarketing drug surveillance mechanism for collecting and reporting data on adverse drug reactions and trends in drug prescribing and usage in the United States.

Wardell has criticized marketing controls because they apply to all physicians without distinction. Thus, medical specialists in university hospitals face the same restrictions as general practitioners. He questions the present method of utilization control over marketed drugs, exerted by the FDA mainly through drug labeling. The FDA should devote more attention to voluntary methods of improving drug utilization, according to Dr. Wardell. Another suggested, more flexible approach would be to implement utilization control

[25]Wardell and Lasagna, *op. cit.*, p. 156.

[26]U.S., Food and Drug Administration, "Clinical Data on New Drugs Generated Outside the United Sates: Proposal to Adopt International Clinical Research Standards," *Federal Register*, Vol. 38, No. 172 (September 6, 1973), pp. 24220-22.

[27]Senator Edward Kennedy, speech before the Annual Pharmaceutical Manufacturers Association Convention, Hot Springs, Virginia, March, 1976.

through third-party payment programs, using the New Zealand and Australia models as prototypes.[28] This type of utilization control can also allow distinctions between physicians of different specialties or levels of training and education, without erecting insurmountable barriers to the treatment of patients with special needs.[29]

SUMMARY

As it has evolved in the United States, governmental controls over drugs have been focused on protecting the public from harm by keeping potentially dangerous drugs off the market. Since 1962, strong federal actions have been instituted to tighten the regulation of pharmaceuticals. The 1962 laws and their interpretation have had mixed results. The same policies that contributed directly or indirectly to the delay in new drug approvals contributed also to the enormous improvement in the standard of investigation for new drugs. Similarly, the delay in the approval of new drugs acts as insurance against hazards subsequently discovered in other countries.

Hence, the current debate is not an all-or-nothing issue; instead, it relates to the relative gains and losses of current government controls. There is a growing body of opinion that the effects of regulation on pharmaceutical innovation and drug utilization are inconsistent with the original intent of Congress. The situation is aptly characterized by Wardell and Lasagna:

> Indeed, if judged by the same standards they themselves set for drugs, the 1962 laws could not be approved because no evidence of their safety or efficacy exists: they were implemented in a scientifically uncontrolled manner, and no measures of their effects were even sought. We are only now beginning to evaluate in retrospect the effects of the changes that began in 1962, and it is doubtful whether their full impact can ever be known."[30]

The essential message is that a more experimental, flexible, and responsive approach is needed to legislate controls in any area beset by so many unknowns. An integral part of a flexible and responsive policy is the continuing, comprehensive evaluation of the gains and losses of drug regulation.

[28]Wardell, "Control of Drug Utilization," *op. cit.*, pp. 585-94.
[29]Wardell and Lasagna, *op. cit.*, p. 153.
[30]*Ibid.*, p. 164.

2
Economic Structure and Performance of the Ethical Pharmaceutical Industry

Jerome E. Schnee
Associate Professor
Graduate School of Business Administration
Rutgers University

Erol Caglarcan
Political Economist
Hoffmann-La Roche Inc.

DEVELOPMENT OF THE ETHICAL PHARMACEUTICAL INDUSTRY

Although disease, infection, and injury are common during periods of peace, they become paramount problems during times of war. Therefore, it is significant to note that past wars have had much influence on the development of the drug industry in the United States. Wars have occasioned extra effort to produce drugs not only because of greater disease and infection and consequent need for medicinals but also because regular sources of supply were usually cut off.[1] For example, the Civil War provided substantial impetus to the development of the American drug industry.[2] The sharp growth in demand for drugs resulted in the founding of E.R. Squibb & Sons; Sharp and Dohme; John Wyeth Company; Parke, Davis & Company; and Eli Lilly and

---

[1] George B. Griffenhagen and James H. Young, "Old English Patent Medicines in America," *The Chemist and Druggist* (June 29, 1957), pp. 717-719.

[2] Glenn Sonnedecker, in the Foreword to *Medicines for the Union Army*, by George W. Smith (Madison: American Institute of the History of Pharmacy, 1962).

23

Company. These firms are among the leading pharmaceutical manufacturers today.

The few important drug discoveries that occurred before the twentieth century included nitrous oxide, ether, and chloroform as anesthetics; amyl nitrite and nitroglycerine for anginal pain; chloral and barbiturate for sedation; and antipyrene, acetanilid, acetophenetidin, and aspirin for the control of pain and fever.[3] Heparin and insulin were discovered in 1918 and 1921, respectively. With rare exceptions, these drugs were good only for relieving symptoms of pain or for inducing sleep.

Salvarsan was one drug which offered more than symptomatic relief in the treatment of syphilis, and with its introduction in 1910, Germany became the center of the pharmaceutical world. However, the outbreak of World War I resulted in the usurpation of Germany's patent rights and signaled the beginning of the growth of the American pharmaceutical industry, as successful duplication of German drugs and processes required American firms to expand existing production and research facilities. Indeed, by the war's end, the United States was providing medical supplies to devastated European countries.

The first of the so-called wonder drugs, sulfanilamide, was discovered in 1935. Until the discovery of sulfanilamide, there was a persistent belief in the medical profession that drugs could not be used to destroy germs within the body. Sulfanilamide belied this myth by effectively treating staphylococcal, streptococcal, and other infections.

World War II greatly increased the use of sulfa drugs and provided the impetus to develop penicillin. The development and large-scale production of penicillin to meet wartime needs began the real transition of the pharmaceutical industry from bulk supplier to finished-dosage form manufacturer. In addition to encouraging research and development of new antibiotic production methods, drug manufacturers had to invest in manufacturing equipment to provide finished drugs to meet military needs. As a result, the compounding function performed by the retail pharmacist had become the province of the manufacturer by the war's end.

After the successful introduction of penicillin, considerable research effort, both publicly and privately supported, was directed to the discovery of other antibiotics which were effective against a much wider range of organisms than was penicillin.[4]

---

[3]Milton Silverman and Philip R. Lee, *Pills, Profits, and Politics* (Los Angeles: University of California Press, 1974), pp.3-4.

[4]The origins and history of the antibiotic industry are documented in *Economic Report on Antibiotics Manufacture* (Washington, D.C.: Federal Trade Commission, June, 1958).

The development of penicillin and the broad-spectrum antibiotics signaled the end of an era in which the industry was composed largely of long-established firms producing relatively standardized pharmaceutical preparations. As new product competition intensified, the industry's expenditures on research and development grew rapidly.[5] For example, between 1951 and 1960, more than 3800 new products and dosage forms were introduced into U.S. pharmaceutical markets.[6] Indeed, it has been estimated that 90 percent of the prescriptions written in 1965 were for drugs unknown in 1950.[7] However, the ratio has dropped sharply in recent years because of the reduced rate of new product introductions since the passage of the 1962 drug amendments.

The post-World War II prosperity of the ethical pharmaceutical industry attracted a host of new firms. There were three distinct characteristics about these newcomers to the industry. Forming the first group of new firms were producers of fine chemicals. These companies had secured wartime contracts to supply drug products in finished form. By the late 1940s, firms such as Merck and Pfizer had emerged as leading producers of drugs, particularly antibiotics.

A second group of entrants included firms known primarily in the proprietary drug field, who either initiated or greatly expanded their activities in the ethical field. The proprietary companies had the advantages of familiarity with production techniques and retail drug distribution, although they had to overcome the longstanding distrust of some physicians toward firms closely identified with patent medicines. Nevertheless, a number of firms with strong proprietary-drug manufacturing background, such as American Home Products and Bristol-Myers, successfully entered the prescription drug market.

Companies with little or no primary relationship to either the ethical or the proprietary fields formed a third category of entrants, which then acquired existing ethical drug firms. An example is Johnson & Johnson, the largest manufacturer of surgical dressings and similar textile products, which acquired McNeil Laboratories in 1959 and has since become a major factor in the oral contraceptive market through its Ortho Pharmaceutical Corporation subsidiary.

[5]For a discussion of the role and function of product differentiation and its relation to research and development activities, see William S. Comanor, "Research and Competitive Product Differentiation in the Pharmaceutical Industry in the United States," *Economica* (November, 1964), pp. 372-384.

[6]Paul de Haen, *New Products Parade* (New York: Paul de Haen, Inc., various issues).

[7]Max Tischler and R.G. Denkewalter, "Drug Research—Whence and Whither," *Progress in Drug Research*, ed. Ernest Jucker (Basel, Switzerland, 1966), p. 12.

MARKET STRUCTURE

The *Standard Industrial Classification (SIC) Manual* classifies drug manufacturing establishments into three industries: biological products, medicinal chemicals and botanical products, and pharmaceutical preparations.[8] The pharmaceutical preparations industry accounts for about 97 percent of all shipments of finished drug products. This industry includes both the ethical drug industry — which provides products only to the medical profession — and the proprietary drug industry — which advertises its products directly to the public. Sales of ethical pharmaceuticals in the United States in 1976 were estimated at $8.7 billion, a level which represents a seventeenfold expansion since the end of World War II.[9]

Since the pharmaceutical industry forms an essential part of the total American health care system, it is instructive to relate industry sales to total health care expenditures. Total U.S. expenditures for health care in 1976 were $139 billion, or 8.6 percent of Gross National Product in 1976.[10] Sales of ethical drugs were equivalent to 6.7 percent of all personal health care expenditures.

The pharmaceutical industry is comprised of several markets, which are essentially therapeutic end-use categories. Since 1962, the Census Bureau has published an annual "Pharmaceutical Preparations" report, based on nine therapeutic classes, including one for veterinary use.[11] However, pharmaceutical preparations for central nervous system and sense organ diseases and for parasitic and infective diseases — the first and second therapeutic categories in sales rank — account for over 40 percent of the total industry sales.

While approximately 600 firms produce prescription products, most of them are small. The *1972 Census of Manufactures* reported that 60 percent had fewer than twenty employees. Although some drug companies are much larger than others, there are no industry-wide, dominant firms such as exist in

[8]U.S., Executive Office of the President, Bureau of the Budget, *Standard Industrial Classification Manual* (Washington, D.C.: U.S. Government Printing Office, 1967) p. 102.

[9]Pharmaceutical Manufacturers Association, *Annual Survey Report: 1975-1976* (Washington, D.C.: PMA, 1976), p.10.

[10]U.S., Social Security Administration, Office of Research and Statistics, "National Health Expenditure Highlights, Fiscal Year, 1976," *Research and Statistics Note*, No. 27 (December 22, 1976).

[11]U.S., Bureau of the Census, "Pharmaceutical Preparations Except Biologicals, 1975," *Current Industrial Reports*, Series MA-28G(75)-1 (August, 1976), p. 1.

Table 1. Domestic Sales by Product Class and Dosage Form for Ethical Drugs for Human Use, 1973-1974 (percentages)[a]

Rank		Dosage-Form Products for	Percentage Share	
1973	1974	Human Use Domestic Sales	1973	1974
1	1	Central nervous system	25.7%	26.5%
2	2	Anti-infectives	16.0	15.9
3	3	Neoplasms and Endocrine system and metabolic disease	11.8	10.1
4	4	Digestives and genitourinary system	11.2	9.9
5	5	Cardiovasculars	8.7	9.1
6	6	Vitamins and nutrients	7.8	8.7
7	7	Respiratory system	6.0	6.4
9	8	Dermatologicals	3.1	3.4
10	9	Biologicals	2.7	2.7
8	10	Diagnostic agents	4.4	2.1[b]
		Other pharmaceutical preparations	2.6	5.2
		Total	100.0%	100.0%

[a] Identical 45 companies, 1973 and 1974.

[b] Includes only *in vivo* diagnostic products. Because of a change in definition introduced in the 1974-1975 survey, sales of *in vitro* diagnostic products are not reported in this table.

SOURCE: Pharmaceutical Manufacturers Association, *Annual Survey Report: 1974-1975* (Washington, D.C.: PMA, 1975), p. 9.

automobiles, steel, or a number of other industries. Moreover, census reports indicate that the four-firm concentration ratio for the ethical pharmaceutical industry declined successively between 1947 and 1958, then again between 1958 and 1967, and was 25 percent in 1972.[12] Among the 408 industries at the SIC four-digit level, 280 (or two-thirds) had higher four-firm concentration ratios than the pharmaceutical industry.[13]

The ethical pharmaceutical market is a dynamic one. Competition results in rapid firm turnover; that is, shifts in market share rankings among the largest firms. Between 1962 and 1972, sixteen of the 21 largest pharmaceutical firms changed market positions. Nine firms improved their market rank, some by eight to ten positions. Twelve firms either failed to improve their market positions or dropped in rankings. The average absolute

[12]U.S., Department of Commerce, Bureau of the Census, *Concentration Ratios in Manufacturing*, MC72(SR)-2, (October, 1975), p. SR2-94.

[13]Pharmaceutical Manufacturers Association, *Prescription Drug Industry Fact Book: 1973* (Washington, D.C.: PMA, 1973), p. ii.

rank change was 4.1 positions (Table 2).[14] Only one industry, petroleum, has higher turnover than the drug industry (Table 3).[15]

Analysis of seventeen therapeutic markets during the 1956-65 decade further illustrates the industry's dynamic market characteristics. The average market share position of the firms ranked first declined from 39.8 percent in 1956 to 14.5 percent in 1965. Similar declines occured for the firms ranked second; their average market position dropped from 15 percent in 1956 to 7.1 percent in 1965.[16]

A further indication of the competitive market structure of the pharmaceutical industry is the entry and exit exhibited within therapeutic submarkets. Between 1963 and 1972 there were more than five successful new entrants in 15 of the 17 product classes analyzed in one study.[17] The average 1972 market share of new entrants exceeded 10 percent with individual market shares ranging as high as 33 and 43 percent (Table 4). Exit occurred in 16 of the 17 therapeutic classes.

Obviously, entry into a therapeutic market could be by entirely new firms from outside the drug industry or by pharmaceutical firms that did not previously market products in that particular market. In either case, the market positions of the existing firms are likely to be affected. New entrants are likely to create additional competition and lower prices. For example, on the basis of his study of the 1963-1972 period, Telser concluded that pharmaceutical prices tend to fall in response to entry of new firms.[18]

[14]Douglas Cocks, "Product Innovation and the Dynamic Elements of Competition in the Ethical Pharmaceutical Industry," *Drug Development and Marketing*, ed. Robert B. Helms (Washington, D.C.: American Enterprise Institute for Public Policy Research, 1975), pp.240-244.

[15]*Ibid*. Data for 19 industries are based on Stephen Hymer and Peter Pashigian, "Turnover of Firms as a Measure of Market Behavior," *Review of Economics and Statistics* (February, 1962), pp. 82-87. Hymer and Pashigian calculated turnover on the basis of shares of assets; the calculation for the drug industry is based on shares of hospital and drugstore sales.

[16]Gordon R. Conrad, "Trends in Market Shares for Ethical Pharmaceutical Products," in U.S., Senate, Committee on Small Business, *Hearings on Competitive Problems in the Drug Industry*, Part 5, 90th Cong., 1st and 2nd Sess., 1968, pp. 1788-1805.

[17]A.T. Kearney, "Study of Economics of Entry and Exit in the Pharmaceutical Industry" (prepared for the Pharmaceutical Manufacturers Association, April 30, 1974).

[18]Lester G. Telser, William Best, John Egan, Harlow N. Higgin Gotham, "The Theory of Supply with Applications to the Ethical Pharmaceutical Industry," *The Journal of Law and Economics* (October, 1975), p.477.

Table 2. Firm Turnover for the Leading 21 Firms in the Ethical Pharmaceutical Industry, 1962-72

Company	Market Share of Hospital and Drugstore Sales (percent of industry total)		Rank in Terms of Market Share		Change in Rank between
	1962	1972	1962	1972	1962 and 1972
Lilly	7.2	7.9	1	1	0
Hoffmann-La Roche	4.0	7.5	10	2	+ 8
American Home Products	6.1	6.6	3	3	0
Merck	4.9	6.0	6	4	+ 2
Bristol-Myers	3.4	4.2	13	5	+ 8
Abbott	3.9	3.7	11	6	+ 5
Pfizer	3.8	3.6	12	7	+ 5
Ciba-Geigy	4.2	3.6	8	8	0
Upjohn	5.8	3.5	4	9	− 5
Squibb	4.1	3.4	9	10	− 1
Smith Kline	6.3	3.3	2	11	− 9
Johnson & Johnson	1.3	2.7	21	12	+ 9
Schering-Plough	2.4	2.7	15	13	+ 2
Parke-Davis[a]	4.6	2.7	7	14	− 7
Searle	2.2	2.5	17	15	+ 2
Lederle	5.3	2.3	5	16	− 11
Sandoz-Wander	1.6	2.0	19	17	+ 2
Robins	1.9	2.0	18	18	0
Sterling	2.4	1.9	16	19	− 3
Burroughs Wellcome	1.4	1.8	20	20	0
Warner-Lambert[a]	2.6	1.7	14	21	− 7
Average absolute change in rank between 1962 and 1972					4.1[b]

[a] Parke-Davis was merged with Warner-Lambert in late 1970; rank and market shares computed as if firms had not merged. Market share of the combined firm in 1972 was 4.4 percent, or fifth in rank.

[b] Computed with Parke-Davis and Warner-Lambert changes based on their ranks as if they had not merged.

SOURCE: D. Cocks, "Production Innovation and the Dynamic Elements of Competition in the Ethical Pharmaceutical Industry," *Drug Development and Marketing*, ed. Robert B. Helms (Washington, D.C.: American Enterprise Institute for Public Policy Research), p. 241.

Table 3. Indices of Market Share Instability

Industry	Instability Index[a]	Number of Firms
Food	10.83	119
Tobacco	9.06	12
Textile mill products	9.30	61
Apparel	1.48	7
Lumber and wood products	4.45	16
Furniture and fixtures	3.86	8
Paper	9.63	49
Printing	14.82	25
Chemicals	17.42	74
Petroleum	24.38	35
Rubber	9.16	14
Leather	5.69	8
Stone, clay, and glass	13.25	31
Primary metals	14.25	76
Fabricated metals	8.70	51
Machinery (except electrical)	12.71	n.a.
Electrical machinery	17.24	46
Transportation	19.92	70
Professional and scientific	17.19	19
Drug industry	22.80	21

[a] All indices are computed with mergers excluded. Hymer and Pashigian calculated their indices on the basis of shares of assets; the calculation for the drug industry by Cocks is based on shares of hospital and drugstore sales.

SOURCE: Stephen Hymer and Peter Pashigian, "Turnover of Firms as a Measure of Market Behavior," *Review of Economics and Statistics* (February, 1962), pp. 82-87 and D. Cocks, *op. cit.*, p. 243.

RESEARCH PERFORMANCE

The research intensity of prescription drug firms is one of the industry's most distinctive economic characteristics. The U.S. ethical pharmaceutical industry annually spends approximately $1 billion for research and development, a twentyfold increase over the last 25 years.[19]

A high proportion of these R & D expenditures is financed by pharmaceutical companies themselves. Less that 1 percent of the pharmaceutical industry's R & D funds is provided by the government as compared to 42 percent for American industry in general. Pharmaceutical manufacturers in the

[19]Pharmaceutical Manufacturers Association, *Annual Survey Report: 1975-1976, op. cit.*, p. 18.

Table 4. Entry into 17 Therapeutic Markets, 1963-1972

Market	Entry Measure 1963-1972[a]	Number of Firms [b]
Anorexics	4.24%	38
Anthelmintics	18.28	4
Antibiotics (B&M)	12.84	56
Anticonvulsants	0.33	7
Antihypertensives	4.85	30
Ataractics	2.63	28
Bronchial dilators	3.76	43
Coronary vasodilators	12.19	43
Diuretics	33.39	19
Oral contraceptives	43.34	6
Oxytocics	1.46	2
Penicillins	7.65	30
Psychostimulants	10.30	9
Sedatives and hypnotics	2.45	39
Sulfonamides	3.17	29
Thyroid preparations	0.44	11
Trichomonacides	16.11	9
Unweighted average	10.44%	

[a] Represents the 1972 market share of successful entering firms that were not in the market in 1963.

[b] Represents the number of successful entrants that make up the entry measure.

SOURCE: Kearney Management Consultants, "Study of Economics of Entry and Exit in the Pharmaceutical Industry," prepared for the Pharmaceutical Manufacturers Association, April 30, 1974, Exhibit II-1.

United States allocate about 11 percent of their net sales to R & D, a figure five times greater than the 2 percent level for U.S. industry as a whole. The drug industry also ranks first in the proportion of its R & D funds allocated to basic research.

The pharmaceutical industry's R & D expenditures are distributed among a wide range of firms of various sizes. Of 70 pharmaceutical companies reporting R & D programs in 1973, 78 percent each invested more than $1 million in R & D activities; and 40 percent each spent $10 million or more. The number of firms with research budgets above $20 million has increased from 8 to 15 between 1968 and 1973.[20]

Many economists have debated the relationship between innovation and firm size in the pharmaceutical industry. Two controversial questions in this regard are: (1) Do large pharmaceutical firms spend more, relative to their

[20]Pharmaceutical Manufacturers Association, *Annual Survey Report: 1973-1974* (Washington, D.C.: PMA, 1974).

size, than small firms on R & D? (2) Do the largest drug firms introduce a disproportionately large share of pharmaceutical innovations? Several economic studies suggest that the answers to these two questions depend on the time period examined; that is, the relationship between innovation and firm size has changed significantly since 1962.

In studies of R & D spending during the 1945-62 period, Mansfield and Grabowski both concluded that the largest drug firms did not spend more on R & D, relative to sales, than did somewhat smaller firms.[21] On the other hand, Schwartzman rejected these earlier conclusions based on his study of the 1965-70 period. Using laboratory employment data, in place of R & D spending data, to measure research effort, Schwartzman found that research effort increases more than proportionally with firm size.[22]

The relationship between pharmaceutical research output and firm size, the second question, has been examined by several investigators. Comanor studied economics of scale in drug research by relating the new drug product output to firm size for the 1955-60 period. He concluded that there were substantial diseconomies of scale in R & D which were associated with large firm size.[23] In a separate study of the most important pharmaceutical innovations introduced between 1935 and 1962, Schnee found that the largest drug firms did not produce a disproportionately large share of the innovations. The pharmaceutical firms that contributed the most innovations, relative to their size, were not the largest firms but somewhat smaller ones.[24]

More recent investigations of technical change and firm size refute the Comanor and Schnee conclusions. For the 1965-70 period, Vernon and Gusen found that larger pharmaceutical firms appeared to have decided advantages over smaller ones in accomplishing technical changes. They disprove Comanor's "diseconomies of scale" hypothesis.[25] Similarly, Schwartzman's study of

[21]Edwin Mansfield, *Industrial Research and Technological Innovation* (New York: W.W. Norton, 1968), pp.38-40; and Henry G. Grabowski, "The Determinants of Industrial Research and Development: A Study of the Chemical, Drug, and Petroleum Industries," *Journal of Political Economy* (March/April, 1963), pp. 292-305.

[22]David Schwartzman, "Research Activity and Size of Firm in the U.S. Pharmaceutical Industry," *Regulation, Economics and Pharmaceutical Innovation,* ed. Joseph D. Cooper (Washington, D.C.: The American University, 1976).

[23]William S. Comanor, "Research and Technical Change in the Pharmaceutical Industry," *Review of Economics and Statistics* (May, 1965), pp. 182-190.

[24]Jerome E. Schnee,"Innovation and Discovery in the U.S. Ethical Pharmaceutical Industry," in E. Mansfield, *et. al., Research and Innovation in the Modern Corporation* (New York: W.W. Norton, 1972), Chapter 8.

[25]John Vernon and Peter Gusen, "Technical Change and Firm Size: The Pharmaceutical Industry," *Review of Economics and Statistics,* 56 (August, 1974), pp. 294-302.

the 1965-70 period leads him to conclude that the largest drug firms produce more innovations, relative to their size, than do smaller ones. Increasing firm size would increase the number of pharmaceutical innovations, according to Schwartzman.[26]

The substantial differences in the findings of the pre-1962 and post-1962 studies strongly suggest that the 1962 amendments to the Food, Drug and Cosmetic Act inadvertently provided an advantage to larger firms, due primarily to the increased costs associated with developing and introducing new drugs since 1962. These huge increases in R & D costs apparently have made it increasingly costly and difficult for small firms to innovate.

PRICING BEHAVIOR

Interest in pricing of ethical pharmaceutical firms dates back to the Kefauver hearings of the late 1950s and early 1960s. A view emerged from these hearings that drug prices did not respond to changes in supply and demand conditions.[27] The criticisms voiced at these hearings and since then involve three separate, but related, issues: (1) the flexibility of individual product prices; (2) the movement of drug prices over time; (3) the price performance of drugs in relation to general price movements.

In a recent study, Cocks and Virts responded to all three of these issues.[28] They noted that a major limitation of earlier drug pricing studies was that the data were obtained from published price lists, which do not reflect the actual prices paid. This finding is similar to the conclusion reached by Stigler and Kindahl on the basis of their study of several industrial markets.[29] They found that published price lists tend to be rigid and do not accurately reflect the behavior of actual transaction prices. For nationally sold products, actual transaction prices tend to be lower and display a much more flexible behavior pattern than catalog prices.[30]

Unfortunately, transaction prices are not readily observable. In order to overcome this methodological shortcoming, Cocks and Virts used actual retail transaction prices of selected prescription drugs to compute retail price in-

[26]Schwartzman, *loc. cit.*

[27]U.S., Congress, Senate, Judiciary Committee, *Administered Prices: Drugs* (Washington, D.C.: U.S. Government Printing Office, 1961).

[28]Douglas L. Cocks and John R. Virts, "Pricing Behavior of the Ethical Pharmaceutical Industry,"*Journal of Business*, 47 (July, 1974), pp. 349-362.

[29]George J. Stigler and James K. Kindahl, *The Behavior of Industrial Prices*, National Bureau of Economic Research (New York: Columbia University Press, 1970).

[30]*Ibid.*

dices. Yet, retail price indices are only an indirect measure of prices charged by the manufacturers. In order to translate the Cocks and Virts findings into conclusions concerning the behavior of pharmaceutical manufacturers' prices, it must be assumed that pharmacists' fees and wholesalers' margins remained essentially constant, which is not an unrealistic assumption. In their study, Cocks and Virts calculated the price changes between 1962 and 1971 for the twelve leading drugs in each of ten product sets and calculated an aggregate price index for each product set. They observed that prices of more than one-half of the product groups declined during this period. The product categories that registered price decreases accounted for approximately 80 percent of all retail prescriptions. The average price decline for the two leading pharmaceutical products in each of the ten categories exceeded 8 percent (Table 5).

Finally, there is considerable evidence that the price performance of pharmaceuticals compares very favorably with changes in general price levels. Between 1967 and June 1977, consumer prices for all items rose by 81.7 percent, while consumer prescription prices increased by only 21.7 percent (Table 6). Most of that increase occurred in line with the severe inflation experienced in 1974 and 1975. Studies conducted by Firestone indicate that the rise in prescription prices is in part due to the increase in the size of the average prescription (Table 7).

The available data indicate that there is much greater price flexibility and price competition in the pharmaceutical industry than has generally been assumed. Competition in prices between several sets of competing drugs has produced a downward trend in prices, relative to other consumer products. Moreover, it has been shown that list price stability is not evidence of lack of competition: A comprehensive review of the economic literature by Demsetz did not reveal any relationship between price changes and market structure.[31]

DRUG INDUSTRY PROFITABILITY

The drug industry is one of the more profitable sectors of the U.S. economy. In fact, in terms of figures found in company annual reports, the rate of return for this industry is higher than it is for most other industries (Table 8). Consequently, questions have been raised regarding the appropriateness of the relative level of drug industry profitability, since profitability rates sometimes have been used in determining the reasonableness of prices.

Therefore, it seems necessary to explain why the accounting rates of return

[31]Harold Demsetz, *The Market Concentration Doctrine: An Examination of Evidence and a Discussion of Policy* (Washington, D.C.: American Enterprise Institute for Public Policy Research, August, 1973).

Table 5. Price Change of Leading Products in Ten Pharmaceutical Markets 1962-71

Percentage Change in Price Index[a]

Rank of Product in Terms of Market Share	Anti-infective	Analgesic and Anti-inflammatory	Psycho-pharmaceutical	Cough and Cold	Anti-hypertensive and Diuretic	Vitamin and Hematinic	Oral Contra-ceptive	Anticholinergic/Antipasmodic	Anti-obesity	Diabetic Therapy
1	− 29.7	− 11.6	− 15.6	+ 10.2	− 8.2	− 3.0	− 19.6	+ 11.9	− 1.3	− 22.0
2	− 6.2	+ 5.1	− 6.8	+ 28.2	− 11.0	+ 12.7	− 9.1	− 6.5	+ 4.1	− 10.0
3	− 66.9	+ 4.5	+ 6.1	− 6.5	− 1.8	+ 4.3	− 8.0	− 1.1	+ 0.5	+ 14.7
4	− 34.4	− 5.0	+ 5.4	+ 37.1	− 0.3	+ 14.7[b]	− 0.7	− 1.4	+ 2.5	+ 1.6
5	− 27.4	+ 9.0	+ 4.2	+ 4.3	− 14.2	− 9.3	− 6.2	+ 6.5	+ 36.8	+ 2.0
6	− 17.9	+ 0.8	+ 5.5	− 3.5	− 11.2	− 8.7	+ 4.3	+ 17.5	+ 5.0	+ 1.3
7	− 32.2	− 10.4	+ 13.2	+ 4.4	− 6.2	− 11.1	+ 10.7	− 1.9	+ 6.1	0
8	− 7.5	+ 8.3	− 35.7	− 0.7	+ 0.8	+ 6.7	+ 14.8	− 0.4	+ 19.4	− 43.5
9	− 52.3	+ 6.5	− 6.0	+ 26.2	+ 1.6	− 13.3	+ 6.2	+ 7.7	+ 2.3	− 23.6
10	− 19.7	+ 8.3	− 10.9	− 4.7	+ 12.5	+ 24.0	+ 3.2	+ 17.8	+ 28.5	+ 1.0
11	− 59.5	− 11.1	—	+ 12.6	− 11.4	− 5.3	+ 0.9	—	—	—
12	− 20.1	− 7.5	—	—	− 8.5	—	—	—	—	—
13	—	—	—	—	− 11.5	—	—	—	—	—
Aggregate price index of leading products	68.2	98.0	91.7	102.9	92.8	99.3	78.0	100.1	105.1	86.3
BLS consumer price index for prescriptions	94.6	94.6	94.6	94.6	94.6	94.6	94.6	94.6	94.6	94.6

[a] Base 1962 or year of introduction if later.

[b] Percentage change for 1962-69 only.

SOURCE: D. Cocks, *op. cit.*, p. 253.

Table 6. Consumer Price Indexes for Selected Components,
1957-1976 (1967 = 100)

Year	All Items	Food	Personal Care	Reading and Recreation	Rx Drugs	All Medical Care
1957	84.3	84.9	84.1	80.4	108.2	69.9
1958	86.6	88.5	86.9	83.9	113.1	73.2
1959	87.3	87.1	88.7	85.3	115.7	76.4
1960	88.7	88.0	90.1	87.3	115.3	79.1
1961	89.6	89.1	90.6	89.3	111.5	81.4
1962	90.6	89.9	92.2	91.3	107.1	83.5
1963	91.7	91.2	93.4	92.8	104.5	85.6
1964	92.9	92.4	94.5	95.0	103.1	87.3
1965	94.5	94.4	95.2	95.9	102.0	89.5
1966	97.2	99.1	97.1	97.5	101.8	93.4
1967	100.0	100.0	100.0	100.0	100.0	100.0
1968	104.2	103.6	104.0	106.2	98.3	106.1
1969	109.8	108.9	109.3	108.7	99.6	113.4
1970	116.3	114.9	113.2	113.4	101.2	120.6
1971	121.3	118.4	116.8	119.3	101.3	128.4
1972	125.3	123.5	119.8	122.8	100.9	132.5
1973	133.1	141.4	125.2	125.9	100.5	137.7
1974	147.7	161.7	137.3	133.8	102.9	150.5
1975	161.2	175.4	150.7	144.4	109.3	168.6
1976	170.5	180.8	160.5	151.2	115.2	184.7

SOURCE: U.S., Department of Labor, Bureau of Labor Statistics.

for this industry are above the average for all industries. Explanations are of two distinct types. Some economists contend that accounting profits tend to overstate the real rate of return in the pharmaceutical industry.[32] They point out that because R & D expenditures are treated as a current expense rather than as an investment, rates of return in drug company financial reports are inflated. For example, on the basis of a comparative analysis of rates of return for drug and other firms, Curley concludes that "conventional accounting procedures necessarily result in biased measures of rates of return."[33]

[32]See for example Harry Bloch, "True Profitability Measures for Pharmaceutical Investment," *Regulation, Economics and Pharmaceutical Innovation,* ed. Joseph D. Cooper (Washington, D.C.: The American University, 1976), pp. 147-156; Robert Ayanian, "Investment in Intangibles and Rates of Return in the Drug Industry," *Drug Development and Marketing,* ed. Robert B. Helms (Washington, D.C.: American Enterprise Institute for Public Policy Research, 1975), pp. 81-96, and Kenneth W. Clarkson, *Intangible Capital and Rates of Return* (Washington, D.C.: American Enterprise Institute for Public Policy Research, 1977).

[33]Baxter and Company, "Comparative Rates of Return for Pharmaceutical and Other Firms: A Conceptual and Empirical Analysis" (Washington, D.C.: Baxter and Company, September, 1974).

Table 7. Firestone Indexes of Wholesale and Retail Pharmaceutical Prices and Adjusted Average Prescription Charge (1967 = 100)

Year	Wholesale (Manufacturer) Prices	Retail (Pharmacy) Prices	Average (Adjusted) Charge
1961	105.2	109.9	105.3
1962	102.2	106.4	103.0
1963	101.2	105.4	102.0
1964	100.8	103.4	101.7
1965	101.2	102.0	101.7
1966	100.8	100.6	101.3
1967	100.0	100.0	100.0
1968	99.1	99.2	99.3
1969	100.1	99.8	100.0
1970	101.0	101.3	101.0
1971	102.9	102.5	102.0
1972	102.4	102.9	101.0
1973	102.7	103.2	99.7
1974	109.3	105.2	102.0
1975	116.2	112.2	109.9
1976	123.8	116.9	113.9

SOURCE: John M. Firestone, "Index of Manufacturers' Prices to Retailers for Ethical Pharmaceuticals, 1976"; "Consumer Price Index for Ethical Pharmaceuticals, 1976"; and "Prescription Size Index, 1976" (May, 1977).

Table 8. Rate of Return on Equity: After Taxes, 1964-1976

Year	All Manufacturing	Drugs and Medicines
1964	11.6	18.2
1965	13.0	20.3
1966	13.5	20.3
1967	11.7	18.7
1968	12.1	18.3
1969	11.5	18.3
1970	9.3	17.6
1971	9.7	17.9
1972	10.6	18.6
1973	13.1	19.2
1974	14.9	18.8
1975	11.5	17.5
1976	13.9	18.0

SOURCE: Federal Trade Commission, *Quarterly Financial Reports*, various issues.

Moreover, this bias is not uniform among industries or even different firms within an industry.

According to Solomon, treatment of intangible assets and depreciation affect reported profit figures. These numbers also depend on the average life of assets, the ratio of working capital to total capital, the time pattern of cash flows, and the firm's growth rate.[34]

Accounting rates of return tend to be most severely overstated in those industries, such as pharmaceuticals, for which research and development constitutes a major proportion of investment outlays. Using a sample of six drug companies, Friedman estimated that capitalization of R & D expenditures would reduce the average rate of return by 4.4 percentage points, thus making the pharmaceutical industry's rate of return more comparable with the similarly adjusted rates of other industries.[35] Therefore, simple comparisons of the type made in Table 8 suffer from various distortions that result from infirmities in accounting conventions.

Researchers have used variables such as risk, growth in demand, and R & D intensity to explore the determinants of an industry's rate of return. In a 1967 study, Conrad and Plotkin found a significant relationship between risk and the rate of return on total capital for companies within 59 industries. The pharmaceuticals ranked fourth in rate of return and fourth in risk. The Conrad-Plotkin model explained a substantial portion of the rate of return differential for drug firms.[36]

Fisher and Hall used a different measure of risk.[37] They measured risk as dispersion of returns over time, as opposed to measuring dispersion across industries as Conrad and Plotkin had done. Nevertheless, both methodologies yielded premiums for risk. The intra-industry comparison showed a risk premium of 8 percent for pharmaceuticals. However, the figure was 1.7 percent when risk was measured as dispersion over time. Conrad and Plotkin pointed out that part of the reason for the discrepancy between the two numbers was that the Fisher-Hall calculations suffered from autocorrelation problems, which reduced the explanatory power of the model.

Similarly, Barges and Hickey identified growth in demand for the industry's products as a significant determinant of return on investment. High

[34]Ezra Solomon, "Alternative Rate of Return Concepts and Their Implications for Utility Regulation," *Bell Journal of Economics and Management* (Spring, 1970), pp. 71-80.

[35]J.J. Friedman and Associates, "R & D Intensity in the Pharmaceutical Industry" (Washington, D.C., September, 1973).

[36]Gordon R. Conrad and Irving H. Plotkin, "Risk/Return: U.S. Industry Pattern," *Harvard Business Review* (March-April, 1968), pp. 90-99.

[37]I.N. Fisher and G.R. Hall, "Risk and Corporate Rates of Return," *Proceedings of the Econometric Society* (December 30, 1973).

growth requires additional capital investment. To attract such capital, higher-than-average returns must be offered; i.e., the "growth premium." In their study, Barges and Hickey attempted to measure the size of this growth premium. However, they were somewhat less successful than Conrad and Plotkin in explaining the drug industry rate of return surplus over the all-manufacturing industry rate.[38]

In a 1974 study, Smith also concluded that the drug industry's higher rate of return reflected both a premium for risk and a premium for growth in pharmaceutical demand.[39]

Recently, concern has been expressed over the drug industry's deteriorating rate of return on R & D investment. Clymer, for example, contends that huge increases in the costs and length of drug R & D and an accompanying decline in new product introductions have combined to sharply reduce the rate of return on R & D investment below 5 percent.[40] Schwartzman estimates that the expected rate of return on R & D investment has declined from 11.4 percent in 1960 to 3.3 percent in 1974. Because the deteriorating rate of return is not likely to attract sufficient future investment in pharmaceutical R & D, Schwartzman advocates that public policy be shaped to encourage profit-motivated R & D.[41] Thomas Stauffer has asserted that the pharmaceutical industry's "phantom rates of return" obscure a deteriorating profitability picture in this industry.[42]

SUMMARY

During the last three decades, the ethical pharmaceutical industry has been transformed into a research-based, highly competitive industry. Sales of ethical drugs in the United States have expanded seventeenfold since the end

[38]Alexander Barges and Brian R. Hickey, "Drug Industry Profits," *Financial Analysts Journal* (May-June, 1968), p. 80.

[39]Rodney F. Smith, "Ethical Drug Industry Return on Investment" (unpublished Ph.D. dissertation, University of Massachusetts, 1974).

[40]Harold A. Clymer, "The Economics of Drug Innovation," *The Development and Control of New Drug Products*, eds. M. Pernarowski and M. Darrach (Vancouver: University of British Columbia, 1972), pp. 121-124.

[41]David Schwartzman, *The Expected Return from Pharmaceutical Research* (Washington, D.C.: American Enterprise Institute for Public Policy Research, 1975), pp.23-42.

[42]Thomas R. Stauffer, "Discovery Risk, Profitability Performance and Survival Risk in a Pharmaceutical Firm," *Regulation, Economics and Pharmaceutical Innovation*, ed. Joseph Cooper (Washington, D.C.: The American University, 1976), pp.93-124.

of World War II, rising to over $6.5 billion in 1974. Manufacturers' sales of ethical drugs were equivalent to 6 percent of all health care expenditures in 1974.

Although there are about 600 firms in the industry, 200 or so enterprises account for 95 percent of total industry sales. On the basis of both concentration and turnover ratios, the ethical pharmaceutical industry is considerably less concentrated than many other U.S. industries. Moreover, there has been considerable entry and exit by firms from within and outside of the pharmaceutical industry into a number of therapeutic markets.

American pharmaceutical firms annually spend approximately $1 billion for research and development, a twentyfold increase over the last 25 years. Recent studies of economies of scale in research have concluded that large pharmaceutical firms have decided advantages over smaller firms in conducting R & D. These findings contrast markedly with the result of studies for the pre-1962 period. The implication is that the 1962 amendments may have inadvertently concentrated pharmaceutical innovation among the larger firms.

Pharmaceutical pricing behavior during the 1960s and 1970s has demonstrated more flexibility and competitiveness than previously had been assumed. One study of prices for 120 leading pharmaceutical products found that the average prescription price declined by more than 8 percent from 1962 to 1971. Another study reported that the retail price of an average prescription in 1976 was 42 cents more than what it was in 1967. This report also indicated that manufacturers' prices rose only 24 percent over this period. During the same period, prices throughout the rest of the economy increased at a much higher rate; general consumer prices by 71 percent and wholesale prices by 83 percent.

The pharmaceutical industry has achieved higher accounting rates of return than most other manufacturing industries. Several analysts have observed, however, that the expensing of R & D expenditures has inflated these accounting rates of return for the pharmaceutical industry. Other economists have attributed some portion of the higher return to risk or growth in pharmaceutical demand. Collectively, these studies explain why the pharmaceutical industry has apparently earned above-average rates of return. However, recent studies conclude that the profitability of investment in pharmaceutical R & D has dropped sharply due to huge increases in the costs and length of new product development and a decline in new drug introductions, suggesting that this situation should be examined from a public policy standpoint.

3

Contributions of the Pharmaceutical Industry to Improved Health

David A. Siskind
Public Policies Analyst
Hoffmann-La Roche Inc.

INTRODUCTION

In any examination of the pharmaceutical industry, one question prevails over all others in singular importance. This question proceeds from the nature of the product the pharmaceutical industy offers and from the business in which the industry is engaged. Unlike many other sectors of our economy, the drug industry is not involved with producing and distributing items of convenience, ease, or luxury. The products of the drug industry are used to cure and prevent disease, alleviate suffering, and sometimes sustain life itself. In short, the business of the drug industry is human health.

This chapter addresses the question of how well the industry has contributed to promoting the public health. The methodology employed involves selectively examining a number of major diseases in the United States and investigating the role of the pharmaceutical industry in helping to combat these diseases (certain benefits of drugs, such as facilitating diagnosis or surgery, are not considered). The impact that the industry's efforts have had is assessed primarily by determining the number and medical value of drugs the industry has produced to fight particular diseases and by reviewing two yardsticks for measuring improvements in the national health; namely, incidence and mortality data for these diseases over time.

It should be emphasized that no claim is being advanced that drugs and drugs alone are the reason for medical progress that has been achieved. Drugs

41

and the industry that produces them are just one part of the overall health care establishment in the United States. This establishment consists of a number of elements, reflecting the fact that the fight against disease is a pluralistic effort, with the pharmaceutical industry being just one significant member of this approach.

Diseases examined have not been those against which the pharmaceutical industry has necessarily had the greatest success, but rather those which have had or are having a major impact on the health of the U. S. population. In this way, an accurate and objective examination of the industry's efforts to improve the national health can be obtained. The diseases considered include infectious diseases, mental illness, cardiovascular diseases, cancer, arthritis, epilepsy, and parkinsonism.

CONTRIBUTIONS OF DRUGS AND THE PHARMACEUTICAL INDUSTRY TO THE NATIONAL HEALTH: AN OVERVIEW

Dr. Philip Lee, former Assistant Secretary of Health for the Department of Health, Education and Welfare, along with his coauthor, pharmacologist Dr. Milton Silverman, has likened drugs to "nuclear weapons" in their "awesome power" and has described their discovery and application as "one of the most exciting chapters in the history of medicine."[1] Similarly, Nobel prize-winning biochemist Ernst B. Chain has labeled drugs as "one of the greatest blessings — perhaps *the* greatest blessing — of our time."[2]

Nonetheless, many tend to take for granted the presence of these chemical substances. A glance back as recently as 40 years ago, however, might sharpen our sense of appreciation. At that time, there were no antibiotics, no corticoids, few sulfa drugs, few vitamins, no tranquilizers, no antihypertensives, no antihistamines, no oral contraceptive drugs, no effective oral diabetic drugs, no prophylactic drugs for gout, no potent active oral diuretics, no drugs to lower the level of blood lipids and cholesterol in the plasma, and no vaccines against polio, measles, or mumps.[3] In short, before development of many of the drugs now available, the human defense against deadly and debilitating diseases was markedly deficient.

Fortunately, great progress has been made. In place of the relatively few drugs available as recently as 1935, there are now hundreds of new chemotherapeutic agents. The originators of new drugs have included

---

[1]Milton Silverman and Philip R. Lee, *Pills, Profits, and Politics* (Los Angeles: University of California Press, 1974), p. xiii.

[2]Ernst B. Chain, "Academic and Industrial Contributions to Drug Research," *Nature* (November 2, 1963), p. 441.

[3]Earle L. Arnow, *Health in a Bottle: Searching for the Drugs that Help* (Philadelphia: Lippincott, 1970), p. 236.

government and academic institutions, private research organizations, and the pharmaceutical industry.

United States sources have been predominant in the discovery of new drugs. In fact, of the 971 new single chemical entities that were developed from 1940 to 1975, 662, or 64 percent, came from the United States. In other words, U.S. sources, including pharmaceutical firms, produced more new drugs than the rest of the world combined.[4] The data also show that pharmaceutical firms (including chemical firms), both domestic and foreign, originated some 828 or roughly 85 percent of *all* the new drugs introduced into the United States during this time period.[5]

These new products helped to revolutionize the treatment and prevention of disease in the United States and contributed to a dramatic improvement in our national health. This improvement is reflected in death rates and life expectancy data covering the past 40 years. The age-adjusted death rate in the United States—which the U. S. Public Health Service considers as one of the most reliable indicators of the nation's health status—declined by almost 47 percent from 1930, from 12.5 per thousand in 1930 to 6.4 per thousand in 1975.[6] Substantial improvement has also been recorded in the life expectancy of the American people. Indeed, as Figure 1 demonstrates, since 1930 more than a decade has been added to the life expectancy of Americans at birth.

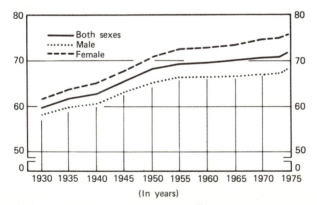

Figure 1. Life expectancy by sex: 1930-1974. [Source: U.S., Department of HEW, Public Health Service, Health Resources Administration, "Final Mortality Statistics, 1974," *Monthly Vital Statistics Report,* Vol. 24, No. 11 (Rockville: National Center for Health Statistics, February 3, 1976), p. 1.]

---

[4]Paul de Haen, "Compilation of New Drugs: 1940 thru 1975," *Pharmacy Times* (March, 1976), p. 41.

[5]*Ibid.*, pp. 46-73.

[6]National Center for Health Statistics (November 4, 1977).

Better nutrition and personal hygiene, better housing and sanitation programs, better overall medical care, and effective drugs have played major roles in improving the health and quality of life of the American people. Together, these are the factors which have significantly improved the national health.

The pharmaceutical industry, in summary, has been a prime source of the new drugs that have become available in the United States. These in turn have contributed to a major improvement in the general health of the U. S. population, as indicated by mortality and life expectancy data and, as will be seen, by examination of specific disease categories.

INFECTIOUS DISEASE

Infectious diseases are caused by invasion into and subsequent multiplication within the human body of foreign organisms, resulting in discomfort, disability, or death. Historically, infectious diseases have been one of man's most deadly enemies. In the United States, for example, and as recently as 1900, just three infectious diseases—influenza, pneumonia, and tuberculosis— accounted for more than 23 percent of *all* deaths recorded.[7] Other infectious diseases which historically have taken a large human toll include mumps, measles, rubella, polio, dysentery, meningitis, syphilis, whooping cough, malaria, small pox, and typhoid fever.

The death rates in the United States for many of these diseases actually began to decline around 1910 as better housing and sanitary conditions became more prevalent. However, beginning in the 1930s major pharmaceutical innovations helped to accelerate this decline, mitigate the debilitating effects of these diseases, and hasten recovery time. These innovations have been basically of two types: curative and preventive. The curative agents consist of the powerful sulfonamides and antibiotics, drugs which possess the ability to attack and kill disease-causing organisms. The preventive agents consist of the vaccines that have been developed to help protect people against contracting certain infectious diseases in the first place.

The sulfonamides, or sulfa drugs, are used primarily to treat infections of the respiratory and urinary tracts, and certain types of meningitis. In an American Medical Association survey of drugs conducted in 1963, the sulfonamides were rated among the most important pharmaceutical advances

---

[7]Odin W. Anderson and Lerner Monroe, *Health Progress in the United States: 1900-1960*, prepared for the Health Information Foundation (Chicago: University of Chicago Press, 1963), p. 16.

since 1934.[8] The first sulfonamide, Prontosil, was discovered in 1932 in the laboratories of a German concern, I.G. Farbenindustrie. Further research has resulted in the availability of 33 new marketed sulfonamides. Of these, 29 or 88 percent have come from the research laboratories of domestic or foreign pharmaceutical firms.[9]

A second major class of drugs essential in combating infectious diseases is the antibiotics, the most famous of which is penicillin. This miraculous substance was discovered in 1928 by an English bacteriologist, Alexander Fleming. It was not until thirteen years later that the first injection of penicillin was administered to a human patient. The man, who lay dying from an infection that developed after he had nicked himself shaving, abruptly began to recover after receiving the drug. However, the process of producing penicillin was so complex that the world's supply of the powerful substance consisted of only a fraction of a teaspoonful. So precious was the substance that traces of it were recovered from the patient's urine in order to stretch the meager supply for as long as possible. In a short time the supply ran out and the patient died.

Mass-production techniques were needed if penicillin were to become a useful medical agent, a need underscored by the outbreak of World War II. Working in cooperation with the U.S. government and British scientists, some twenty American pharmaceutical concerns challenged extremely complex engineering and technical problems to devise a means of producing penicillin in quantity. Combined, these forces expended $28 million, $25 million of which was spent by the drug firms.[10] This effort led to major new engineering techniques permitting the large-scale production of penicillin. Thus, a major laboratory discovery became generally available as a therapeutic agent.

The mass production of penicillin coincided with the discovery of another significant antibiotic, streptomycin, by Selman Waksman of Rutgers University. Working closely with Dr. Waksman, Merck & Company developed a production process for streptomycin which included strain and culture-medium improvement and the elaboration of extraction and purification methods of the substance, which was insoluble in all the usual organic solvents. Through the Merck effort an important laboratory discovery became a useful and available therapeutic agent.

The drug industry has not merely supplied the technical expertise to

[8]Pharmaceutical Manufacturers Association, *Prescription Drug Industry Fact Book: 1968* (Washington, D. C.: PMA, 1968), pp. 44-45.

[9]de Haen, *op. cit.*, p. 54.

[10]Wyndham Davies, "Before and After the Pharmaceutical Revolution," *The Pharmaceutical Industry: A Personal Study* (Oxford: Pergamon Press, Ltd., 1967), p. 5.

translate research discoveries into available products, as important as this contribution is. The industry has also discovered important antibiotics such as chlortetracycline, the first broad-spectrum antibiotic — effective against both gram-positive and gram-negative bacteria. Discovered in 1946 by Lederle Laboratories, chlortetracycline was found to be active against another group of microorganisms called rickettsia, which causes diseases such as typhus and Rocky Mountain spotted fever. This drug paved the way for many further discoveries. Indeed, it proved to be only the first of an entire group of powerful antibiotics known as the tetracyclines. The tetracyclines, like the sulfonamides, are considered to be among the most significant pharmaceutical advances since 1934.[11] They are used in the treatment of a wide variety of diseases caused by many different types of microorganisms.

Other important contributions in the field of antibiotics include the isolation in the 1940s by Parke-Davis of chloramphenicol and the discovery by Hoffmann-La Roche of the effectiveness of isoniazid in the treatment and prophylaxis of tuberculosis. Isoniazid has had a major impact in the decline in mortality and incidence rates for tuberculosis. Both chloramphenicol and isoniazid are recognized by the AMA as also being among the most important therapeutic advances since 1934.[12] The pharmaceutical industry has also helped develop such groups of antibiotics as the macrolides, the polymyxins, and synthetic penicillins. This last group has proven to be especially important in light of the capability of certain bacteria to develop a resistance to natural penicillin and also because the new penicillins possess improved properties.

Overall, the pharmaceutical industry (domestic and foreign) is responsible for originating 48 of the 51 (94 percent) broad- and medium-spectrum antibiotics that were available as medical agents in the United States as of 1975, and for isolating a forty-ninth. Additionally, 28 of the 33 (or 85 percent) different types of penicillin and derivatives available originated in industry laboratories.[13]

Vaccines are a third major contribution to the control of infectious diseases. For example, the polio vaccines have very nearly eliminated this once-dreaded disease as a health problem or cause of death, as can be seen in Figure 2. While Drs. Jonas Salk and Albert Sabin deserve the greatest credit for their magnificent work in this effort, the contributions of drug firms are often overlooked. Researchers at Parke-Davis, for example, were the first to take close-up photographs of isolated polio viruses. Scientists at Lederle

---

[11]Pharmaceutical Manufacturers Association, *loc. cit.*

[12]*Ibid.*

[13]de Haen, *op. cit.*, pp. 50-52.

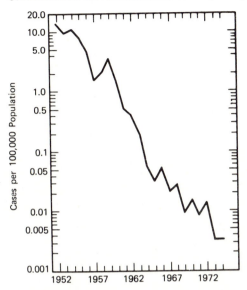

Figure 2. Poliomyelitis (paralytic)-reported cases per 100,000 population by year, United States, 1952-1974. [Source: U.S., Department of HEW, Public Health Service, Health Resources Administration, *Health, United States, 1975,* (HRA) 76-1232 (Rockville: National Center for Health Statistics, 1975), p. 269.]

Laboratories were among the first to devise an experimental, live-virus polio vaccine capable of being ingested by human patients.

Today, our supply of the polio vaccine is manufactured by pharmaceutical producers. A number of drug companies also make vaccines against mumps, measles, and rubella. Additionally, the pharmaceutical industry, in conjunction with the U.S. Public Health Service, was primarily responsible for the development of vaccines against whooping cough and certain types of influenza.

The impact of the sulfonamides, antibiotics, and vaccines on our nation's health has been dramatic, as demonstrated in Table 1, which compares death rates from selected infectious diseases for the period 1920 to 1975. The impact of these drugs and vaccines can also be assessed by comparing incidence rates for several highly communicable diseases over the period 1950 to 1976 (Table 2).

As these tables indicate, fewer people die from or contract debilitating infectious diseases. This produces a substantial economic benefit for the nation, in terms of fewer lost workdays, reduced use of such medical facilities as hospital beds and in-patient services, and better utilization of our finite medical resources. More importantly, though, this progress means that

Table 1. Death Rate per 100,000 Population

Causes of Death	1920	1930	1940	1950	1960	1975	Decline, 1920-1975
Tuberculosis, all forms	113.1	71.1	45.9	22.5	5.9	1.6	98%
Dysentery	4.0	2.8	1.9	0.6	0.2	0.0[a]	100%
Whooping cough	12.5	4.8	2.2	0.7	0.1	0.0	100%
Meningococcal infections	1.6	3.6	0.5	0.6	0.3	0.1	100%
Diphtheria	15.3	4.9	1.1	0.3	0.0[b]	—	100%
Measles	8.8	3.2	0.5	0.3	0.2	0.0	100%
Influenza and pneumonia	207.3	102.5	70.3	31.3	36.6	26.1	88%

[a] Bacillary dysentery and amebiasis.

[b] 1959 (figures for 1960 and 1975 not available).

SOURCE: Ernst B. Chain, "Academic and Industrial Contributions to Drug Research," *Nature* (November 2, 1963), p. 441; and U.S., Department of HEW, Public Health Service, Health Resources Administration, "Final Mortality Statistics, 1975," *Monthly Vital Statistics Report*, Vol. 25, No. 11 (Rockville: National Center for Health Statistics, February 11, 1977), p. 16.

Table 2. Reported Cases of Specified Notifiable Diseases, 1951 to 1976

Diseases	1951	1960	1965	1976	Decline, 1951 to 1976
Measles (rubeola)	530,118	441,703	261,904	41,126	92%
Meningococcal infections	4,164	2,259	3,040	1,605	61%
Mumps	n.a.[a]	n.a.	152,109[c]	38,492	75% (from 1968)
Whooping cough	68,687	14,809	6,799	1,010	99%
Poliomyelitis	28,386	3,190	79	14	99%
Rubella (German measles)	n.a.	n.a.	45,975[d]	12,491	73% (from 1966)
Tuberculosis	85,607[b]	55,494	48,016	32,105	62%
Typhoid fever	2,128	816	454	419	80%

[a] n.a. = not available.

[b] 1952 figure (1951 not available).

[c] 1968 figure (not previously reportable).

[d] 1966 figure.

SOURCE: U.S., Department of HEW, Public Health Service, "Reported Morbidity and Mortality In the United States, 1976," *Morbidity and Mortality Weekly Report*, Vol. 25, No. 53 (Atlanta: Center for Disease Control, August, 1977), p. 2; and U.S., Department of HEW, Public Health Service, "Annual Reported Incidence of Notifiable Diseases In the United States, 1960," *Morbidity and Mortality Weekly Report*, Vol. 9, No. 53 (Atlanta: Communicable Disease Control, October 30, 1961), p. 4.

significant numbers of people have been protected from disease. Pharmaceuticals are one of several factors that have contributed substantially to this achievement.

MENTAL ILLNESS

Unlike some infectious diseases, mental illness is not typically a fatal disease. Yet this sickness, whether mild or severe, can involve much suffering and incapacitation, taking such forms as depression, schizophrenia, or other types of psychoneurotic and psychotic disturbances. Mental illness or other personality disturbances are not infrequently factors in delinquency, suicide, alcoholism, addiction, or criminal behavior, and may also contribute to certain physical illnesses, including heart disease.[14] Mental illness is a disease more prevalent in this country than most people may realize. In 1973, more than 4.5 million Americans required assistance of some sort in mental health facilities.[15]

The pharmaceutical industry has helped to improve the quality of care received by the mentally ill. Since the 1950s the industry has introduced a number of tranquilizing, antianxiety, and antidepressant drugs which affect the central nervous system. Such drugs have proven to be of critical value in treating mental illness and, like other pharmaceuticals already mentioned in this chapter, are considered by the AMA to be among the most significant therapeutic advances of recent decades.[16]

The discovery of tranquilizers was actually a by-product of industrial research on antihistamines. Researchers at the Rhone-Poulenc Company in France observed that certain of their experimental antihistamines possessed pronounced sedative properties. A systematic attempt was undertaken, therefore, to modify the structure of the antihistamines in order to intensify their sedative properties. These efforts led to the discovery of chlorpromazine, the first effective "major" tranquilizer, in 1954.

The effects of chlorpromazine on mental patients were pronounced. As one expert has observed:

> Patients who paced in rooms with no furniture to smash or toilets to stuff with rags or clothes, who tore on the plaster on the walls, glared and shouted at nothing real — became calm. Other patients who lived so deeply within their own

---

[14]National Health Education Committee, *Facts on the Major Killing and Crippling Diseases in the United States Today*, (New York: National Health Education Committee, 1966), p. 1.

[15]U.S., Department of HEW, Public Health Service, Health Resources Administration, *Health, United States, 1975, op. cit.*, p. 321.

[16]Pharmaceutical Manufacturers Association, *loc. cit.*

private dream worlds that communication was impossible became accessible so that psychiatric treatment could be carried out.[17]

The introduction of chlorpromazine was followed by another major therapeutic advance when scientists at Hoffmann-La Roche, led by Dr. Leo H. Sternbach, succeeded in synthesizing chlordiazepoxide hydrochloride. This so-called "minor" tranquilizer was found capable of exerting antianxiety action but without substantial effect on the autonomic nervous system. In other words, the drug was effective in controlling certain psychoneurotic disorders, but with little interference with human consciousness and activity. Shortly thereafter, Roche discovered diazepam, an effective agent for relief of tension and anxiety, as well as muscle spasms and convulsions.

In all, since 1954, the drug industry has been primarily responsible for the origination and development of 51 of the 56 new ataraxics introduced into the United States through 1975.[18] Table 3 profiles some of the major therapeutic advances used in the control of mental illness.

Tranquilizers and antidepressant drugs have exerted a substantial positive impact on the treatment of mental illness in the United States. For example, in 1956, two years after the introduction of chlorpromazine, the population of mental hospitals in the United States declined for the first time in 175 years. Not only has this decline continued, but since 1964 with respect to state and county mental hospitals, it has decreased at a steadily faster rate each year (see Figure 3). According to Drs. Earl Pollack and Carl Taube of the National Institute of Mental Health, there is "no question" that this decline has been due to the "widespread introduction of psychoactive drugs into the mental hospitals."[19]

It is not unlikely that the introduction of these drugs has contributed further to increasing release among admissions to state mental hospitals at earlier points in time. A study of the probability of release among first admissions to eleven state mental hospital systems in 1954 found a range of 14 to 53 percent released within the first three months after admission and 29 to 68 percent within the first six months. Although there are no comparable data on first admissions for the same states for a later period, a sample survey of total admissions to state mental hospitals in 1971 revealed that 75 percent were released within the first three months and 87 percent within the first six months.[20]

[17]Arnow, op. cit., p. 56.

[18]de Haen, op. cit., p. 56.

[19]Earl S. Pollack and Carl A. Taube, "Trends and Projections in State Hospital Use," speech presented at the symposium on "The Future Roles of the State Hospital," Division of Community Psychiatry, State University of New York, Buffalo, New York, October 11, 1973.

[20]Ibid.

Table 3. Major Drugs for Control of Mental Illness

Drug Product	Source of Innovation	Introducing Firm to U.S.	Year of Introduction
Chlorpromazine	Rhone Poulenc	Smith Kline & French	1954
Trifluoperazine	Smith Kline & French	Smith Kline & French	1958
Thioridazine	Sandoz (Switzerland)	Sandoz	1959
Chlordiazepoxide	Hoffmann-La Roche	Hoffmann-La Roche	1960
Diazepam	Hoffmann-La Roche	Hoffmann-La Roche	1963

SOURCE: Harbridge House, Inc., *Innovation In the Pharmaceutical Industry and Its Social Benefits* (Boston: Harbridge House, Inc., December 31, 1971), p. 46.

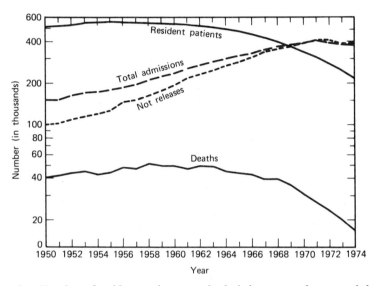

Figure 3.   Number of resident patients, total admissions, net releases, and deaths, state and county mental hospitals, 1950-1974. [Source: U.S., Department of HEW, Public Health Service, *Health, United States, 1975*, (HRA) 76-1232 (Rockville: National Center for Health Statistics, 1975), p. 317.]

Tranquilizers and antidepressants have also facilitated home treatment of the mentally ill. In 1955, 77.4 percent of all patients treated for mental illness needed in-patient service. By 1973, this percentage had dropped to 35.3 percent. Correspondingly, the percentage of mentally ill who have been able to receive treatment outside the hospital — and thus remain with their families and not infrequently maintain their normal activities — has increased from 22.6 percent in 1955 to 64.7 percent in 1973. Table 4 details the progress made in this regard.

In summary, pharmaceuticals have had a pronounced effect on the treat-

Table 4. Number, Percent Distribution, and Rates per 100,000 Population of Inpatient and Outpatient Care Episodes in Selected Mental Health Facilites, by Type of Facility: United States 1955, 1965, 1967, 1969, 1971 and 1973

			Inpatient Services of:						Outpatient Psychiatric Services of:		
Year	Total Facilities	Total Inpatient	State and County Mental Hospitals	Private Mental Hospitals	General Hospital Psychiatric Service (non-VA)	VA Psychiatric Inpatient Services	Federally Assisted Cmty. Mental Health Centers	Total Outpatient	Federally Assisted Central Health Center	Other
	Number					*Percent distribution*					
1973	4,749,362	100.0	35.3	13.7	3.2	10.0	4.4	4.0	64.7	20.7	44.0
1971	4,038,143	100.0	42.6	18.5	3.1	13.4	4.4	3.27	57.4	15.4	42.0
1969	3,572,822	100.0	47.0	21.5	3.5	15.0	5.2	1.8	53.0	8.1	44.9
1967	3,139,742	100.0	52.9	25.5	4.0	18.4	4.1	0.9	47.1	8.1	44.0
1965	2,636,525	100.0	59.4	30.5	4.8	19.7	4.4	—	40.6	—	40.6
1955	1,675,352	100.0	77.4	48.9	7.3	15.9	5.3	—	22.6	—	22.6
						Rate per 100,000 population					
1973	—	2282.4	807.2	313.3	73.0	228.5	100.2	92.2	1475.2	472.2	1003.0
1971	—	1981.5	847.2	364.9	66.1	265.7	86.9	63.7	1134.3	305.0	823.3
1969	—	1797.7	849.6	384.2	62.0	268.2	93.6	41.7	948.1	145.2	802.9
1967	—	1604.3	847.9	409.5	63.5	295.6	65.5	13.8	756.4	49.7	706.7
1965	—	1374.0	815.9	419.5	65.4	270.6	60.4	—	558.1	—	552.1
1955	—	1032.2	798.6	504.5	75.9	163.8	54.5	—	233.5	—	233.5

Omitted from this table are: private psychiatric orfice practice; psychiatric service modes of all types in hospitals or outpatient clinics of Federal agencies other than the V.A. (e.g., Public Health Service, Indian Health Service, Department of Defense, Bureau of Prisons, etc. inpatient service modes of multi-service facilities not shown in this table; all partial care episodes, and outpatient episodes in V.A. hospitals.

Includes estimates of episodes of care in residential treatment centers for emotionally disturbed children.

SOURCE: U.S., Department of HEW, Public Health Service, Health Resources Administration, *Health, United States, 1975* (HRA) 76-1232 (Rockville: National Center for Helath Statistics, 1975), p. 321. Outpatient data may also reflect changing fiscal policies, including Medicaid, Medicare, and other forms of insurance.

ment of mentally ill patients in the United States. They have provided relief from mental suffering for literally millions of people. This is partially reflected in the sharp decrease in the population of mental hospitals and in the earlier release times and shorter treatment periods for those afflicted. It is further reflected in the fact that the treatment of the mentally ill may now take place more frequently within the home, where patients may remain with their families and often maintain jobs and other productive activities.

CARDIOVASCULAR DISEASES

The greatest killers today are cardiovascular diseases, diseases of the heart and blood vessels. Major diseases of the cardiovascular system include hypertension (high blood pressure), arteriosclerosis (hardening of the arteries), heart attack, stroke, congestive heart failure, and rheumatic heart disease. The American Heart Association estimates that about 29 million Americans suffer from cardiovascular diseases, as indicated in Figure 4. Mortality data indicate that more people in the United States die from cardiovascular diseases than from all other causes of death combined. In 1973,

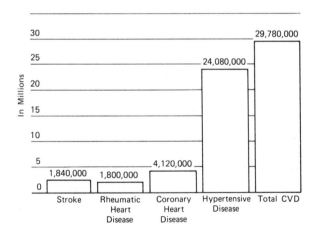

Figure 4. Estimated prevalence of the major cardiovascular diseases, United States, 1975. *Note:* The sum of the individual estimates exceeds 29,780,000 (total CVD) since many persons have more than one cardiovascular disorder. [Source: American Heart Association, *Heart Facts, 1978* (New York: American Heart Association, 1977)].

for example, 1,037,460, or 52.4 percent of the 1,970,000 total deaths recorded in the United States were caused by cardiovascular diseases.[21] Table 5 offers mortality figures for major cardiovascular diseases in the United States over the period 1950-1973.

Discouraging as they are, these incidence and mortality figures might have been much worse were it not for the progress that has been achieved over the past 25 years in the field of cardiovascular medicine. Understanding of cardiovascular diseases has increased significantly, and this has led to substantial improvements in the ability to diagnose, prevent, and treat cardiovascular diseases. The pharmaceutical industry has been a part of this progress.

Indicative of the industry's contribution has been the development of anticoagulant drugs, therapeutic agents that inhibit blood clotting. These drugs have proven to be of value in treating certain forms of heart disease, as well as dangerous clotting conditions of the veins. Progress also has been made in developing drugs which can actually dissolve existing clots, although their use is not as yet widespread. Overall, eleven major anticoagulant drugs have been discovered, developed, and made available in the United States since 1942. Table 6 indicates the role of the pharmaceutical industry in this endeavor.

The discovery of new and effective diuretics, drugs that remove fluid from body tissues, is another major advance in the field of cardiovascular medicine. These drugs are particularly useful in combating congestive heart failure. The first major diuretic, chlorothiazide, was introduced in 1957 by Merck Sharp & Dohme after 14 years of research. Since 1943, 36 diuretics have been added to the arsenal against cardiovascular disease and 35 of these were originated, developed, and introduced by pharmaceutical companies.[22]

Industry has also helped to develop drugs that can reduce levels of cholesterol and other fatty substances in the blood. These drugs are thought to be particularly useful in the treatment of arteriosclerosis. Better control over blood pressure has been achieved by the development of such drugs as vasodilators and antihypertensives, which are used to lower dangerously high blood pressures, and vasoconstrictors to raise dangerously low pressure. Overall, the drug industry originated seven of eight vasoconstrictors introduced into the United States since 1940, 18 of 21 antihypertensives, and 10 of 17 vasodilators.[23]

The industry has been especially active in producing antibiotics which have

---

[21]U.S., Department of HEW, Public Health Service, Health Resources Administration, "Annual Summary for the United States, 1973, Births, Deaths, Marriages, and Divorces," *Monthly Vital Statistic Report*, Vol. 22, No. 1 (Rockville: National Center for Health Statistics, June 27, 1974), p. 20.

[22]de Haen, *op. cit.*, p. 65.

[23]*Ibid.*, pp. 60-62

Table 5. Deaths in the United States from Cardiovascular Diseases, 1950-1973[a]

	1973	1970	1965	1960	1955	1950
Number of deaths from all causes	1,970,000	1,921,031	1,828,136	1,711,982	1,528,717	1,452,454
Percentage of all deaths caused by cardiovascular Disease	52.4	52.4	54.1	53.9	53.3	51.3
Major cardiovascular diseases	1,037,460	1,007,984	990,192	123,635	815,532	745,074
Diseases of heart	754,460	735,542	712,087	661,712	585,751	537,629
Active rheumatic fever and chronic rheumatic heart disease	13,584	14,889	15,471	18,411	19,757	22,316
*Hypertensive heart disease	13,200	14,991	54,968	66,308	73,883	85,193
Ischemic heart disease	682,910	666,665	559,293	494,282	405,830	336,619
*Chronic disease of endocardium and other myocardial insufficiency	4,870	6,705	53,178	57,029	65,622	85,159
All other forms of heart disease	34,900	32,292	29,177	25,682	20,659	23,958
Hypertension	8,010	8,273	11,667	12,662	11,162	12,563
Cerebrovascular diseases	214,650	207,166	201,057	193,588	174,142	156,751
Arteriosclerosis	33,430	31,682	38,102	35,876	32,486	30,734
Other diseases of arteries	26,910	25,321	27,279	19,797	11,991	7,397

[a]It should be noted that in 1968, the United States adopted a new disease classification system. Thus, the exact definition of specific disease categories may have changed beginning in 1968 and this, of course, could produce different data results. In most cases, however, the comparability ratios between disease classifications before and after 1968 are great enough to permit valid comparison of the data. The two exceptions to this rule are noted by an asterisk on the chart.

SOURCE: U.S., Department of Public Health Service, Health Resources Administration, "Annual Summary for the United States, 1973, Births, Deaths, Marriages, and Divorces, "Monthly Vital Statistics Report, Vol. 22, No. 1 (Rockville: National Center for Health Statistics, June 27, 1974), p. 20; and U.S., Department of Public Health Service, Health Resources Administration, "Mortality Trends for Leading Causes of Death, United States—1950-1969," Vital and Health Statistics, Series 20, Number 16 (Rockville: National Center for Health Statistics, March, 1974), pp. 62-63.

helped to combat rheumatic heart disease and to prevent certain kinds of heart infections. For example, subacute bacterial endocarditis, a severe infection of the heart lining, has become quite uncommon as a result of the wide availability of antibiotics. The industry also has developed drugs that have helped to control such cardiovascular ailments as arrhythmias and to treat angina pectoris, often a precursor of heart attack.

Table 6. Anticoagulants

Marketed	Trademark	Generic Name	Originator	Developer
1942	Heparin	heparin sodium	McLean, Johns Hopkins Univ. (U.S.)	Upjohn; various manufacturers
1944	Dicumarol	dicumarol	Wisconsin Alumni Foundation (U.S.)	Various manufacturers
1950	Tromexan	ethyl biscoumacetate	Unknown (Czechoslovakia)	Geigy
1951	Cumopyran	cyclocumarol	Univ. of Wisconsin (U.S.)	Abbott
1952	Hedulin	phenindione	Oberval (France)	Walker (Merrell-Nat'l)
1954	Coumadin	warfarin sodium	Univ. of Wisconsin (U.S.)	Endo
1955	Dipaxin	diphenadione	Upjohn (U.S.)	Upjohn
1957	Sintrom	acenocoumarol	Geigy (Switzerland)	Geigy
1958	Liquamar	phenoprocoumon	Hoffmann-La Roche (Switzerland)	Organon
1960	Athrombin-K	warfarin potassium	Univ. of Wisconsin (U.S.)	Purdue Frederick
1960	Miradon	anisindione	Schering (U.S.)	Schering

SOURCE: Paul de Haen, "Compilation of New Drugs: 1940 thru 1975," *Pharmacy Times* (March, 1976), p. 48.

Advancements such as these—combined with other factors such as improved diet and physical exercise programs, better emergency and surgical procedures, and greater awareness of the signs of potential cardiovascular problems on the part of individuals—have had a definite positive impact. Despite the mortality and incidence figures reported above, the data indicate that the *rate* of Americans dying from cardiovascular diseases has actually begun to decline. This death rate climbed steadily during the 1950s and early 1960s, reaching a peak of 521.3 per 100,000 in 1963. Since then, however, the death rate for cardiovascular disease has dropped to 494.4 per 100,000, a decline from 1963 of more than 5 percent (see Table 7). This decline has occurred despite the large increase in that segment of the American population over 45 which is most susceptible to cardiovascular diseases.

As Table 7 shows, most of the other disease categories comprising the general cardiovascular disease group have also exhibited declining rates of death. Some of these declines have been quite significant. The death rate from rheumatic fever and heart disease has dropped 37 percent since 1960; from hypertension, 46 percent; and from arteriosclerosis, 20 percent. Since 1968, when a new classification system went into effect, the death rate from hypertensive heart disease has declined 20 percent and from chronic disease of endocardium and other myocardial insufficiency, 41 percent.

Table 7. Death Rates for Cardiovascular Diseases, 1960-1973 (per 100,000)[a]

	1960	1961	1962	1963	1964	1965	1966	1967	1968	1969	1970	1971	1972	1973	% Change from 1960
All major cardiovascular diseases	515.1	505.1	515.1	521.3	508.5	510.9	516.1	506.5	512.1	501.7	496.0	491.9	493.9	494.4	-4.0%
Diseases of the heart	369.0	362.4	370.1	375.2	365.7	367.4	371.2	364.5	372.6	366.1	362.0	359.5	361.3	359.5	-2.5%
Active rheumatic fever and chronic rheumatic heart disease	10.3	9.8	9.5	8.8	8.3	8.0	7.7	7.2	8.2	7.6	7.3	7.1	6.8	6.5	-37.0%
Hypertensive heart disease with or without renal disease	37.0	34.6	33.4	34.4	30.0	28.4	27.7	25.3	8.9	8.1	7.3	6.8	6.3	6.3	-32.0%* (from 1968)
Ischemic heart disease	275.6	274.4	283.8	289.8	285.0	233.5	292.7	289.7	337.6	331.7	328.1	326.1	328.0	325.4	+35.3%
Chronic disease of endocardium and other myocardial insufficiency	31.5	29.3	29.4	29.7	27.8	27.4	27.4	26.6	3.9	3.7	3.3	3.0	2.6	2.3	-41.0%* (from 1968)
All other forms of heart disease	14.3	13.8	13.9	14.5	14.5	13.1	15.9	15.8	14.0	15.0	15.9	16.6	17.7	19.0	+32.8%
Hypertension	7.1	6.7	6.7	6.7	6.4	6.0	5.8	5.6	4.5	4.2	4.1	3.8	3.7	3.8	-46.4%
Cerebrovascular diseases	108.0	105.4	106.2	106.6	103.6	103.7	104.6	102.2	105.8	102.6	101.9	101.1	100.9	102.3	-5.2%
Arteriosclerosis	20.0	19.3	19.8	19.8	19.4	19.7	19.9	19.0	16.8	16.4	15.6	15.2	15.8	15.9	-20.5%
Other diseases of arteries, arterioles and capillaries	11.0	11.3	12.2	12.9	13.5	14.1	14.6	15.1	12.4	12.4	12.5	12.2	12.3	12.8	+15.3%

[a]Beginning in 1968, the U.S. adopted the Eighth Revision of the International Classification of Diseases. For most categories this revision did not significantly affect calculation of death rates. For the *categories, however, the discontinuity between the seventh and eighth revisions was great enough so as to render impractical comparisons between pre-1968 and subsequent data.

SOURCE: U.S. Department of HEW, Public Health Service, Health Resources Administration, "Annual Summary for the United States, 1973, Births, Deaths, Marriages, and Divorces," *Monthly Vital Statistics Report*, Vol. 22, No. 1 (Rockville: National Center for Health Statistics, June 27, 1974), pp. 20-21; and U.S. Department of HEW, Public Health Service, Health Resources Administration, "Mortality Trends of Leading Causes of Death, United States, 1950-1969," *Vital and Health Statistics*, Series 20, Number 16 (Rockville: National Center for Health Statistics, March, 1974), pp. 60-61.

These data are encouraging, and they reflect the progress made in combating cardiovascular diseases, with drugs being a significant factor contributing to this progress. There is little doubt, however, that cardiovascular diseases remain our principal enemies. The challenge then confronting the health care establishment in this country is to continue its efforts to find new treatments, methods for earlier diagnoses, and cures for cardiovascular diseases. For its part, the drug industry in 1976 devoted over $100 million to cardiovascular research.[24]

CANCER

Second only to cardiovascular disease in its lethal impact on the American people is cancer. Cancer is actually a generic term referring to several hundred different diseases characterized by the production of malignant or abnormal cells in the body which multiply and spread without regard to normal body regulatory mechanisms. The American Cancer Society reports that there were an estimated 370,000 cancer deaths in 1976 and forecasts 390,000 deaths in 1978.[25]

More than one million Americans are under medical care for cancer. An estimated 675,000 developed some form of cancer during 1976 and another 385,000 are expected to contract cancer during 1978.[26] Table 8 reflects the impact of cancer in the United States by estimating cancer deaths and *new* cases in 1978.

The origins of cancer still largely elude medical science and its treatment constitutes a major medical challenge. However, therapeutic procedures have been developed which involve surgery, radiation therapy, hormones, and drugs.

Hundreds of drugs have been synthesized in the fight against cancer. Certain of these, roughly forty, are now being marketed commercially, and most have come from pharmaceutical industry laboratories.[27] Other drugs remain classified as experimental. Together with other forms of treatment, these drugs have helped to lower the death rates of persons stricken with cancer. In

[24]PMA estimate, report November 7, 1977.

[25]American Cancer Society, '76 *Cancer Facts and Figures* (New York: American Cancer Society, 1975), p. 4; conversation with an official of the American Cancer Society, September 27, 1977.

[26]*Ibid.*, p. 6.

[27]de Haen, *op. cit.*, p. 57.

Table 8. Estimated New Cases and Deaths for Major Sites of Cancer, 1978[a]

Site	Number of Cases	Deaths
Lung	102,000	92,400
Colon-rectum	102,000	51,900
Breast	91,000	34,100
Uterus	48,000[b]	10,700
Oral	24,000	8,400
Skin	9,600[c]	5,600
Leukemia	21,500	15,100
Prostate	57,000	20,600

[a] Figures rounded to the nearest 1000.

[b] If carcinoma-in-situ included, cases total over 87,000.

[c] Estimated new cases of non-melanoma skin cancer about 300,000.

Incidence rates are based on rates from N. C. I. Third National Cancer Survey 1969-71.

SOURCE: Conversation with an official of the American Cancer Society, September 27, 1977.

the 1930s, fewer than one in five cancer patients was alive at least fives years after diagnosis. Now one in three is alive at five years. Expressed in more appreciable terms, the gain from one in five to one in three represents about 90,000 lives each year.[28]

One type of cancer in which treatment with drugs has yielded promising results is leukemia, a cancer of the blood-forming tissues.[29] It involves the abnormal production of immature blood cells and the interruption of the vital blood-forming functions of the bone marrow. In all, as Table 8 indicates, 21,500 Americans will be stricken by leukemia in 1978. Some 15,100 will die.

One of the most rewarding breakthroughs in leukemia research occurred in 1947, when Dr. Sidney Farber of the Children's Cancer Research Foundation discovered that a substance, aminopterin, caused temporary remissions in acute childhood leukemia. This discovery was based on experimental evidence that folic acid, a so-called cellular metabolite, stimulates the acute leukemia process. Research chemists from Lederle Laboratories synthesized a number of folic acid antagonists, and their efforts led to the discovery that aminopterin and its less toxic successor, methotrexate, caused temporary remissions in leukemia patients.

In 1952, another collaborative effort between clinicians and pharmaceutical research scientists resulted in the discovery of another leukemia

[28]American Cancer Society, *op. cit.*, p. 3.

[29]This account is based on a report by the Pharmaceutical Manufacturers Association entitled "Pharmaceutical R&D Contributes to Advances in Treatment of Leukemia," *PMA Commentaries* (Washington, D.C.: PMA, November, 1975), pp. 7-10.

drug, 6-mercaptopurine. Chemists at the Wellcome Research Laboratories, who had been studying nucleic acids for nearly ten years, finally synthesized 6-mercaptopurine and began testing its effect, first on animal tumors and later on cancer patients. The first remissions were reported in 1953 by J.H. Burchenal and his colleagues at the Sloan-Kettering Institute. Subsequent clinical trials confirmed that 6-mercaptopurine could produce remissions in a number of patients with acute leukemia.

Since these initial discoveries, further research has led to the introduction of additional anti-leukemia drugs. Today there are more than ten drugs used alone or in combination that may induce complete remission of acute leukemia. Some patients may remain in remission indefinitely. These drugs, along with the pharmaceutical firms that have played major roles in either their origination or development, include: methotrexate (Lederle), 6-mercaptopurine (Burroughs-Wellcome), thioguahine (Burroughs-Wellcome), prednisone (Schering), cyclophosphamide (Asta-Werke), vincristine (Lilly), and cytosine arabinoside (Upjohn).

The impact of these drugs is demonstrated by the fact that chemotherapy (the chemical treatment of cancer) has become the primary means of controlling leukemia. Before Dr. Farber's pioneer use of aminopterin in 1947, physicians attempted with little success to control the production of leukemic cells with radiation alone. By 1970, however, radiation as the sole means of treatment had decreased to 1 percent of leukemia cases treated while drug therapy as the sole means of treatment increased to 70 percent.[30]

A more important measurement of the impact of chemotherapy is the survival rate for those afflicted with leukemia. A survey of 100 U.S. hospitals indicated that between 1940-1949 and 1965-1969, the percentage of patients with acute leukemia who survived for one or more years increased from 5 to 37 percent.[31] With respect to forms of leukemia afflicting children, by 1960, enough progress had been made to allow a few patients to live five years. Today, with a remission rate in these forms of leukemia of about 90 percent and a steadily increasing first remission duration, approximately 25 percent of patients diagnosed this year will be alive for at least five years.[32]

Cancer experts are optimistic that greater progress is in the making. They predict that as new drug therapies are used more widely, there will be a dramatic improvement in the national death statistics from leukemia.[33] For example, medical centers specializing in acute leukemia studies are projecting

[30]*Ibid.*, p. 9.

[31]*Ibid.*, p.7.

[32]*Ibid.*, p. 7.

[33]"Gaining on Death: Drugs are Emerging as Powerful Weapons for Fighting Cancer," *Wall Street Journal* (April 1, 1976), p. 1.

a 50 percent five-year survival rate in adults.[34] Moreover, with regard to childhood leukemia particularly, certain cancer centers are reporting that more than half of the children treated experimentally with a regimen of drugs have passed the five-year mark alive and free of their disease—and many are well and disease-free after ten years.[35]

Hodgkin's disease is another form of cancer against which drugs have helped to make significant progress. The incidence of this disease is relatively small, with about 7000 new cases estimated in 1976. However, Hodgkin's disease has traditionally been considered important because, although not always fatal, its death rate claims one out of every two afflicted and because many of its victims are young adults with their productive lives ahead of them.[36]

Though its origins are still not completely understood, Hodgkin's disease has yielded to recent advances in therapy. The five-year survival rate for persons with the disease rose from 25 percent in the 1940s to 54 percent in the 1960s.[37] The three-year survival rate has risen over the past twenty years from 35 to 61 percent.[38] Greater progress is indicated by a National Cancer Institute study in which 80 percent of 193 Hodgkin's disease patients treated five years ago or more with a variety of drugs have had complete remissions of their cancer.[39] One of the most effective forms of treatment is a so-called MOPP program developed by the National Cancer Institute. The program takes its name from the first letters of the four drugs it employs. Three of these four drugs were originated by pharmaceutical concerns: oncovin (Lilly); procarbazine (Hoffmann-La Roche); and prednisone (Schering). The fourth drug, mechlorethamine, resulted from work done by the University of Leeds in Britain.

Drugs also show promise of constituting an effective anticancer aid in cancer of the breast. In 1974, 32,424 Americans, mostly women, died from breast cancer.[40] Hope for improvement is contained in the preliminary results

[34]Pharmaceutical Manufacturers Association, "Pharmaceutical R&D Contributes to Advances in Treatment of Leukemia," *op. cit.*, p. 7.

[35]*Wall Street Journal, op. cit.*, p. 20.

[36]American Cancer Society, *op. cit.*, p. 9.

[37]*Ibid.*, p. 7.

[38]Roche Laboratories, "Hodgkin's Disease," *Roche Research in Cancer, Past, Present, and Future*, Report prepared for Roche Laboratories, Division of Hoffmann-La Roche Inc., Nutley, New Jersey, 1975, p. 18.

[39]*Wall Street Journal, loc. cit.*

[40]U.S., Department of HEW, Public Health Service, Health Resources Administration, "Final Mortality Statistics, 1974," *Monthly Vital Statistics Report*, Vol. 24, No. 11 (Rockville: National Center for Health Statistics, February 3, 1976), p. 1.

of a study being conducted using a combination of three drugs as postoperative therapy. Investigators have been able to reduce the recurrence of breast cancer after surgery among these high-risk patients. Patients receiving the drug combination showed a cancer recurrence rate of only 5.4 percent, compared to 24 percent for those not receiving the drugs.[41]

Pharmaceutical concerns helped in originating and developing the three drugs — cyclophosphamide, 5-fluorouracil, and methotrexate — employed in the study. Cyclophosphamide was originated by the German firm of Asta-Werke and developed in the United States by Mead Johnson. Hoffmann-La Roche, in collaboration with the University of Wisconsin, was primarily responsible for the origination and development of 5-fluorouracil, a drug also used to treat cancer of the colon, rectum, stomach, and pancreas. Methotrexate was developed by Lederle Laboratories.

In summary, the pharmaceutical industry has, either through its own efforts or in collaboration with other research organizations, discovered, developed, and distributed important anticancer drugs. It continues to study and investigate many others, working closely with hospitals and cancer centers throughout the nation. Much work remains to be done before treatment procedures will be available which will lead to major reductions in cancer mortality. Ideally, however, drugs will someday be available to treat cancer in much the same way as antibiotics and vaccines are now used to combat infectious diseases.

OTHER MAJOR DISEASES

Arthritis

Arthritis is one of the most common diseases in the United States today. In its 1975 report on *Health In the United States*, the Department of Health, Education and Welfare states that arthritis is the most prevalent chronic condition reported in interviews among the civilian noninstitutionalized population of the United States.[42]

The Arthritis Foundation estimates that some 50 million people — nearly one quarter of the entire U.S. population — have arthritis to some degree. As noted in Table 9, approximately 20 million of these are afflicted seriously enough to necessitate medical care.

Drugs have proven to be a valuable medical tool in the treatment of pa-

---

[41]"Drugs Found Supplement to Breast Cancer Surgery," *New York Times* (February 18, 1976), p. 1.

[42]U.S., Department of HEW, Public Health Service, Health Resources Administration, *Health, United States, 1975, op. cit.*, p. 246.

Table 9. Arthritis Victims Needing Medical Care

Rheumatoid arthritis	5,000,000
Osteoarthritis	12,000,000
Arthritis in children	250,000
Gouty arthritis	1,000,000
Other arthritis forms	2,000,000
TOTAL	20,250,000

SOURCE: The Arthritis Foundation, *The Arthritis Foundation 1976 Annual Report* (New York: Arthritis Foundation, 1977), p. 2.

tients suffering from arthritis. Primarily, these drugs provide symptomatic relief from the pain and inflammation associated with the disease. Among the most widely used agents in this regard are the steroid hormones, the most notable of these being cortisone.

The introduction of cortisone in 1950 climaxed years of cooperation between university and industrial research laboratories. In 1935, Dr. Edward C. Kendall of the Mayo Clinic in Minnesota succeeded in obtaining a few microscopic granules of a substance he had isolated and labeled as "compound E." This compound was a steroid, that is, a substance like hormones and other important body chemicals which are built around rings of atoms. But, compound E was so complex that synthesis seemed utterly hopeless and, as a result, the substance was largely ignored. In 1941, however, rumors reached the Defense Department that Nazi pilots were able to fly at tremendously high altitudes after being injected with certain hormones. Though the rumors proved false, they prompted an intensive research effort in the United States.

In 1946, after years of frustrating research, Merck & Company succeeded in performing the first practical synthesis of compound E, by this time known as cortisone. The synthesizing process was extraordinarily complex, involving thirty-three steps. Eventually, however, it was perfected and a certain amount of cortisone was sent to Dr. Philip S. Hench, also of the Mayo Clinic, who believed the substance could be useful in the treatment of rheumatoid arthritis.

Dr. Hench's belief proved to be well-founded. The experimental drug was injected into a bedridden woman crippled with arthritis. A week later, she was out shopping. Cortisone thus became the first breakthrough in the treatment of rheumatoid arthritis. Subsequently, however, cortisone's use had to be restricted due to troublesome side effects.

There have been other significant advances, including hydrocortisone, prednisone, triamcinalone and dexamethasone. Overall, since 1940, 32 new "corticoids" have been introduced into the United States, with the drug industry playing a principal, if not exclusive, role in the origination of all of them.[43]

Joining these drugs in the treatment of arthritis have been nonhormonal agents such as probenecid, developed by Sharpe and Dohme in 1952, and allopurinol, developed by Burroughs-Wellcome in 1966. Presently there are nine such antiarthritics available in the United States, all having originated from drug industry laboratories.[44]

Another group of nonhormonal, antiinflammatory agents has become a cornerstone in the treatment of arthritis. About 15 years ago Merck discovered indomethacin, which was quite effective in the treatment of many forms of arthritis and yet was free of cortisone's major adverse effects. There are presently six nonhormonal, antiinflammatory agents available in the United States, four of which resulted from industry research.[45] Many others are currently in development.

Arthritis remains a major disease afflicting millions of Americans. Considerable medical progress has been made, however, in discovering drugs that can alleviate the pain and suffering associated with the disease. Their medical value is attested to by the AMA survey, which included the corticoids in the class of drugs ranked second only to the penicillins in terms of pharmaceutical importance.[46]

Parkinsonism

Parkinsonism is a term applied to chronic neurological disorders which are characterized by progressive muscular rigidity, tremors, and loss of automatic associated movements. An official of the U.S. Public Health Service estimates that between a million and a million-and-a-half Americans suffer from various forms of parkinsonism and that 50,000 more are afflicted each year.[47]

The precise cause of parkinsonism is not known and no preventive or curative agent yet exists. However, progress has been made recently in understanding the disease and in developing the means to substantially alleviate the symptoms of parkinsonism. This progress has resulted from cooperative efforts of several dedicated scientists both inside and outside the pharmaceutical industry. Their efforts led to the introduction of a drug

[43]de Haen, *op. cit.*, pp. 69-70.

[44]*Ibid., p. 48.*

[45]*Ibid.*, p. 54.

[46]Pharmaceutical Manufacturers Association, *Prescription Drug Industry Fact Book: 1968, op. cit.*, pp. 44-45.

[47] Conversation with Ms. Reday, Public Information Officer of the U.S., Department of HEW, Public Health Service, Washington, D.C., February 5,1976.

called levodopa, considered to be among the most important advances in the field of neurology.

Levodopa (also known as L-dopa) is a naturally occurring substance that was first isolated in 1913 by Hoffmann-La Roche. It was not until the 1960s, however, that research results strongly suggested that L-dopa could be useful in treating parkinson patients. Studies indicated that in the brain the levels of a naturally occurring substance called dopamine were markedly reduced in individuals suffering from Parkinson's disease. Dopamine was believed to be a "neurotransmitter," that is, a substance produced by the human body to help transmit commands within the nervous system. The low levels of dopamine in parkinson patients, it was theorized, could be associated with the muscular disability characteristic of parkinsonism.

Attempts to use dopamine itself to treat Parkinson's disease proved unsuccessful because dopamine was not able to pass from the blood into the brain, that is, to penetrate the so-called blood-brain barrier. Its chemical precursor, levodopa, however, not only penetrated the blood-brain barrier, but also converted into dopamine within the brain. By 1968, Dr. George Cotzias of Brookhaven National Laboratories proved that the treatment of parkinsonism with large doses of levodopa by mouth was possible.

A more intensive and more coordinated study was necessary, however, in order to understand more fully the properties and usefulness of the substance in combating parkinsonism. As a result, Hoffmann-La Roche, in cooperation with NIH and prominent neurologists, launched a major multicenter clinical evaluation of levodopa. In 1970 the Food and Drug Administration approved the use of levodopa in the treatment of Parkinson's disease. Continued research on ways to improve levodopa has already produced significant results. Merck, for example, has introduced a drug product that combines levodopa with a substance called carbidopa. This combination allows less levodopa to be used in treatment and reduces the adverse side effects of levodopa.

Epilepsy

Epilepsy, a disorder of the central nervous system, involves a recurrent loss or impairment of consciousness which, in turn, may be accompanied by muscular movements ranging from slight twitching of the eyelids to convulsive shaking of the entire body. Though only very rarely a cause of death, epilepsy is usually a long-term chronic disease with the vast majority of seizures starting in childhood or adolescence. An estimated 4 million Americans suffer from the disease.[48]

[48]Greater New York Chapter, Epilepsy Foundation of America, *Answers to the Most Frequent Questions People Ask About Epilepsy* (Washington, D.C.: Epilepsy Foundation of America, November, 1973), p. 9.

The specific cause of epilepsy is not known, nor has a cure been found. However, a number of antiepileptic drugs have been developed which, for not completely understood reasons, inhibit the sudden bursts of electricity that cause epileptic seizures and thus help to control convulsions (see Table 10). Most of these originated in industrial research laboratories.

Through the use of these anticonvulsive drugs, over 50 percent of persons with epilepsy can completely control their seizures and live active, seizure-free lives. They can attend school, hold a full-time job, and raise a family. Another 30 percent, moreover, can gain significant control of their seizures.[49] In other words, the majority of epileptics are now able to assume many of the responsibilities of the ordinary healthy person.

CONCLUSION

At the beginning of this chapter we asked how well the pharmaceutical industry had contributed to promoting the public health. The answer is that few other sectors of our society—private or public—have exerted such a beneficial impact on our lives. Even critics of the industry support this view. Drs. Silverman and Lee, for instance, in their book *Pills, Profits, and Politics*, recognize that "few if any other industries have contributed so magnificently to the health and welfare of the public, to the control of pain and sickness, and to the prolongation of life."[50]

Table 10. Anticonvulsants

Trademark	Generic Name	Year of Introduction	Originator
Dilantin	diphenylhydantoin	1938	Parke-Davis
Tridione	trimethadione	1946	Abbott
Mesantoin	mephenytoin	1947	Sandoz
Paradione	paramethadione	1949	Abbott
Phenurone	phenacemide	1951	Abbott
Milontin	phensuximide	1953	Parke-Davis
Mysoline	prinidone	1954	ICI
Celontin	methsuximide	1951	Parke-Davis
Zarontin	ethosuximide	1960	Parke-Davis
Tegretol	carbamazepine	1975	Ciba-Geigy
Clonopin	chlorazepam	1975	Roche

SOURCE: National Health Education Committee, *Facts on the Major Killing and Crippling Diseases In the United States Today* (New York: National Health Education Committee, 1966), p. 3; and Paul de Haen, "Compilation of New Drugs: 1940 thru 1975," *Pharmacy Times* (March, 1976), p. 48.

[49]National Health Education Committee, *op. cit.*, p. 3.

[50]Silverman and Lee, *op. cit.*, p. 24.

In certain respects, the industry's contributions can be quantitatively measured. For example, as noted earlier, approximately 85 percent of all the new drugs discovered and introduced in the United States since 1940 have come from pharmaceutical companies. These medicines extend across a broad spectrum of therapeutic uses. From pharmaceutical industry research, for example, have come 88 percent of our presently available sulfonamides, 94 percent of our broad- and medium-spectrum antibiotics, 85 percent of our synthetic penicillins, 86 percent of our antihypertensives, 88 percent of our vasoconstrictors, 65 percent of our vasodilators, most of our marketed cancer drugs, and nearly all of our corticiods and antiarthritics.[51] The drug industry also helped to originate and develop vaccines used effectively against once-dreaded infectious diseases such as polio, mumps, and measles.

The industry's contribution can further be gauged by examining mortality and incidence data for major diseases. As this chapter has shown, dramatic progress has been made in reducing the number of people dying from or contracting infectious diseases. With respect to such diseases as cancer and heart disease, where tremendous challenges remain, progress has been made in reducing death rates and improving survival prospects. For still other diseases, like mental illness, arthritis, parkinsonism, and epilepsy, pharmaceuticals have helped to alleviate symptoms and mitigate adverse effects.

Finally, a portion of the industry's contribution lies beyond quantitative assessment. Numbers cannot really measure the relief from pain and sickness enjoyed by a single individual, nor can statistics honestly gauge the enhanced quality of life permitted by a healthy existence. Herein are more subtle but no less important contributions of the pharmaceutical industry to our health. They are manifested not in statistics, but in more rewarding personal lives, happier family lives, and more productive professional lives. They are manifested in lives freer from disease.

---

[51]Data based on the list compiled by de Haen, *op. cit.*, pp. 69-70.

4
Pharmaceutical Marketing

Gilbert D. Harrell
Associate Professor of Marketing and Transportation Administration
The Graduate School of Business
Michigan State University

INTRODUCTION

The pharmaceutical industry places unique demands on the role of marketing. The nature of the product requires that firms interact with many heterogeneous publics, including highly educated professionals faced with important tasks. Pharmaceuticals are only a part of society's basic health support system, and their use is affected by many factors. Ultimately, patient benefits from pharmaceuticals accrue from proper diagnosis, prescribing, manufacture, distribution, and consumption. It is a highly personal form of business where accuracy in meeting a consumer's needs is of prime importance. Each purchase decision can be instrumental to the health of the patient, and yet the dollar cost of that decision may be low compared to other purchases of lesser importance. This chapter describes the role of pharmaceutical marketing in the delivery of drugs.

Salient marketing functions in the pharmaceutical industry include: sales,* advertising, marketing research and planning, and support services to health care professionals. Sales and advertising have received most of the attention in the literature, which is to be expected given the magnitude of investments for these functions and because they are inherently more visible than the other functions. According to an industry source, the 1975 direct outlay for medical journal advertising, direct mail advertising, and detailing was $508 million, invested by pharmaceutical firms to promote approximately 3000 medicines

---

*In the pharmaceutical industry, selling is often referred to as detailing, and sales representatives commonly are referred to as detailmen.

to 355,000 practicing physicians.[1] Additionally, 116,000 dentists and 121,000 pharmacists require marketing efforts.[2] Most of the current expenditures are for the introduction of new products, new dosages, and new medical uses as well as the marketing of older products. Marketing activities must be viewed in a setting of rapid new product introduction, new technical knowledge, and continuous product obsolescence. Pharmacists, wholesalers, retailers, and patients all play a part in marketing success; yet the major marketing efforts are aimed at the relatively small and precisely defined group of highly educated prescribers who, for the most part, have veto power over each product. Because the physician market is clearly defined, identifiable, and relatively compact, it provides excellent conditions for marketing/promotional efforts.

While pharmaceutical marketing efforts are instrumental in directing the relationship of the firm with its many customers, these activities are also among the most regulated for any industry. Aside from the conventional legal restrictions observed by all industries, the Food and Drug Administration closely regulates advertising and promotion content and practices, drug development, introduction, and distribution. Additionally, the nature of its products subjects the pharmaceutical industry to constant public scrutiny.

In a nutshell, pharmaceutical marketing must strive to inform a technically sophisticated audience about dramatically changing product and service mixes in a climate of constant governmental regulation, public scrutiny, and industry competition.

THE PHYSICIAN MARKET

The natural place to begin an in-depth discussion of marketing in any industry is where it has the largest impact, with the customers. In the pharmaceutical industry, the customers are the physicians. Therefore, to grasp the nature of pharmaceutical marketing, it is necessary to understand the nature of the physician community. This chapter discusses only the broad dimensions of this market. Of more importance perhaps is a description of how pharmaceutical firms assess physicians' needs. For marketing success it is essential to understand and predict prescribers' needs and to develop products to satisfy those needs.

---

[1]IMS America, Ambler, Pennsylvania. Another source, however, has estimated a higher figure: $768 million in 1973. FDC Reports, Inc., "The Pink Sheet," *FDC Reports* (Washington, D.C.: FDC Reports, Inc., August 20, 1973). For more cost data, see p. 79.

[2]*Indicia*, February/March, 1976.

Physician Population

Although the physician population is the most important target for marketing effort, it is far from homogeneous in pharmaceutical requirements. Table 1 indicates the range of specialties.

What might appear to be a relatively compact group of prescribers, when only their number — 355,000 — is considered, becomes on closer examination highly divergent, highly segmented groups of specialists. Physicians often possess subtle divergent predispositions and attitudes toward a particular drug. There are not only varying arrays of diseases among patients but also vast differences in the diseases treated across specialties. Furthermore, the training of physicians by specialty affects prescribing. "Shotgun" marketing programs (which are low cost initially) often simply do not communicate with a wide range of doctors at an accurate and beneficial level. Rather, more personalized and direct ("rifle") communication messages and channels are required. To complicate further any analysis of the product, physician specialty, and patient condition profile process, many drugs have multiple indications. The results can be that for very legitimate reasons different doctors

Table 1. Physicians by Specialty

Allergy	2,130
Anesthesiology	13,841
Cardiovascular	6,749
Dermatology	4,707
Emergency medicine	2,123
Gastroenterology	2,237
General practice	59,170
Internal medicine	57,753
Neurology	4,168
Obstetrics and gynecology	22,480
Occupational medicine	2,312
Ophthalmology	11,412
Ear-nose-throat	5,892
Pathology	12,676
Pediatrics	22,994
Psychiatry	27,762
Pulmonary disease	2,263
Radiology	17,203
Surgery	53,174
Urology	6,917
Other and unspecified	16,897
Total Physicians	354,860

SOURCE: *Indicia* (February/March, 1976).

prescribe the same drug for different actions or that the same doctor prescribes a single drug for different actions. When physiological differences among patients are considered, the outcome may be that a doctor prescribes different products for the same indications in different patients or, in some cases, for the same patient. Of course, one could also take into account dosage schedules, dosage forms, price, and prescription sizes. In the final analysis it is clear that effective communication with physicians requires an enlightened and sensitive marketing specialist.

Market Research

Advances in marketing research have aided in creating a more efficient marketing system. Numerous pharmaceutical manufacturer employees and specialists from outside firms are engaged in the process of assessing physician needs, wants, attitudes, and prescribing behaviors. Several research firms specialize solely in pharmaceutical usage audits and prescriber behavior studies. Among the tools and techniques employed are computer simulations, attitude measurement models, multidimensional scaling, and market testing. The primary objective of marketing research is to provide information that will enhance communications with physicians by obtaining feedback on the wide range of activities performed by the firm. Comprehensive marketing information systems supply the feedback necessary to improve the allocation of marketing resources.

PHYSICIAN PRESCRIBING BEHAVIOR AND THE EFFECTS OF COMMUNICATION

Knowledge concerning the relationship between marketing expenditures and their effects on physicians' prescribing practices are imprecise at best. No published studies adequately document the cost-benefit ratio in this area, but a series of research reports have examined how physicians value and use varying sources of information about pharmaceuticals, irrespective of relative costs. This type of information provides the necessary insight into prescribing behavior on which are based important implications regarding marketing efforts. Of course, the best way to assess the impact of promotion is to analyze the role of all information in physician prescribing decisions. This ideal has not yet been achieved, but several studies (approximately twenty published since 1940) have attempted to understand the importance of various types of commercial and noncommercial information. The following is a brief summary of some of the research conducted during the last fifteen years.

Information Sources

What sources of information are most important to physicians: pharmacists, colleagues, patients, journal and professional articles, journal advertising, direct mail, or sales representatives? The answer depends on several factors, including the type of information sought; the newness of the drug; the severity of the drug's therapeutic indication; and the training, experience, and predisposition of the physician. Most evidence suggests that all of these sources interact to provide the medical community with a dynamic and readily available bank of information. All relevant published data on the subject support the conclusion that marketing information is an important factor in keeping physicians informed.[3]

Most work to date has investigated only one type of information, that concerning new drugs. Little is known about marketing information and its use in decisions regarding older products.

Based on rather limited evidence, sales representatives and journal articles seem to be the most influential sources in keeping physicians informed.[4] Direct mail is next in importance, followed by information from colleagues. One of the older studies in this field found that commercial sources predominate but do not overwhelm other sources as a means of making the physician aware of new drugs. This study also reported that physicians attach no stigma to the use of commercial information.[5]

Most physicians indicate that sales representatives are a source of data—among other commercial promotional means—on which they tend to rely, particularly for learning about new drug products. For example, an AMA survey of its members in 1973 indicated that over 50 percent believed that sales representatives had a "marked" or "moderate" influence on their prescribing patterns. This compares to about 25 percent, who felt they were influenced by pharmaceutical advertising in medical journals, and 17 percent, who felt they were influenced by direct mail promotions. In contrast, the highest percentages by far claimed they were influenced by the *Physicians' Desk Reference* (84 percent) and by the recommendations of other doctors (79 percent).[6]

[3]R. A. Bauer and L. H. Wortzel, "Doctor's Choice: The Physician and His Sources of Information About Drugs," *Journal of Marketing Research*, VIII (February, 1966), pp. 40–47.

[4]Charles Winick, "The Diffusion of an Innovation Among Physicians in a Large City," *Sociometry*, 4 (December, 1961), pp. 384–396; and James S. Coleman, Elihu Katz, and Herbert Menzel, *Medical Innovation: A Diffusion Study* (New York: Bobbs-Merrill, 1966).

[5]Ben Gaffin and Associates, *Attitudes of U.S. Physicians Toward the American Pharmaceutical Industry* (Chicago: Ben Gaffin and Associates, 1959).

[6]American Medical Association, *Opinions of AMA Members, 1973*, report prepared by the Center for Health Services (Chicago: American Medical Association, 1973).

Winick conducted an elaborate study of physicians' interpersonal professional contacts and commercial sources in the adoption of a new drug, Chemneo, a new and distinctive addition to a growing drug class. He concluded that

"physicians who were slow in trying Chemneo differ from more rapid adopters in their tendency to pay some heed to non-professional sources, while the more rapid adopters seem to be more sensitized to professional sources . . . . For all groups, however, the rational commercial sources of journals and detailmen seem to be the most important source of information about a new drug."[7]

Physician Confidence and Risk Perception

An element that probably mediates the value of information from various sources is the physician's perception of the risk of prescribing a product and his or her subjective confidence in estimating the effects of its use.[8] It appears that physicians use more information from noncommercial sources (and, in some cases, commercial sources) when the risk of prescribing increases. The less certain they are regarding salient consequences, the greater the search for information.

In 1973, Dennis B. Worthen reviewed most of the literature in the United States and the United Kingdom regarding information sources as they related to physician prescribing behavior. While research on the subject is far from definitive, he concluded:

The commercial influences — representatives (detailmen), journal advertising and direct mail — serve as a channel to inform the physician of the existence of the product and the information needed to prescribe for it. This information includes dosage forms, dose, side effects and contraindications as well as the indications for the product's use.

The pharmacist appears to be an overlapping channel with commercial influences.

The professional sources — the physician's peer group and professional journals — do not appear to have an important function as far as informing the physician of product availability. Instead they function as a legitimizing chan-

[7]Charles Winick, loc. cit.

[8]Raymond A. Bauer, "Risk Handling in Drug Adoption: The Role of Company Preference," Public Opinion Quarterly; Gilbert D. Harrell, "Modeling Physician Prescribing Behavior: Attitudes, Normative Beliefs, Motivation to Comply, Confidence, Behavioral Intention and Behavior" (unpublished Ph.D. dissertation, The Pennsylvania State University, 1972); and Peter D. Bennett and Gilbert D. Harrell, "The Role of Confidence in Understanding and Predicting Buyers' Attitudes and Purchase Intentions," Journal of Consumer Research (1975).

nel and influence prescribing habits by bestowing some form of approval in the physician's use of a product.[9]

Clearly, marketing efforts do play a role in informing physicians and, therefore, influence prescribing behavior. These efforts operate through a nexus of interpersonal channels as well as directly on the physician. In practice, most major manufacturers coordinate detailing, direct mail, journal advertising, and sampling to communicate relatively homogeneous messages about individual products. The effects of each promotional effort can vary widely, and the value to the physician is dependent on a number of factors, including the nature of his practice, his background, the ease of contact with other physicians, and the riskiness of the prescribing situation.

More is known about the magnitude of marketing activities involved in product planning, promotion, and distribution than about the effects of these activities on physician prescribing behavior. The marketing activities that facilitate successful delivery of pharmaceuticals are discussed next.

PRODUCT DECISIONS

Historically, new product introductions to expand the spectrum of disease treatments have played a major role in improving health care and have provided the single largest growth opportunity for most firms. Almost all marketing activity has been toward the introduction of these single new pharmacological entities. The pharmaceutical industry, unlike other industries, funds nearly all of its own R&D activities.

Research and development and new product introduction are risky; success or failure to return a profit is determined by the physician market. The physician's experience and knowledge ultimately judges the merits of a drug. All of this occurs in an environment where knowledge and techniques of medical science are developing, and hence the merits of specific drugs can be perceived differently as new evidence surfaces. In general, physicians view the marketing efforts of manufacturers as an important means of keeping abreast of the evolutionary volume of new and highly technical product information.[10] For manufacturers, the ability to promote new products and present new evidence using their own marketing teams assures them a means of securing physicians' reactions and possible drug trial and adoption.

---

[9]Dennis B. Worthen, "Prescribing Influences: An Overview," *British Journal of Medical Education*, Vol. VII (1973), pp. 109-117.

[10]R. A. Bauer and L. H. Wortzel, *loc. cit.*

Breadth of Product Lines

An analysis of the top 21 producers indicates that most large firms have a relatively broad product line, the majority having entries in over 50 percent of all therapeutic categories (see Table 2). This broad product base allows varying competitive actions and fluctuating market shares. Douglas L. Cocks[11] has computed a market share instability index based on the earlier work of Hymer and Pashigian.[12] Of 20 major industries, only the petroleum industry has more market share instability than did these 21 firms in the pharmaceutical industry. While the index is an imprecise measure of competitive action, it does indicate that leadership in pharmaceuticals is often in flux.

Most product classes have several competitors vying for market share. Table 3 shows the sales volume and number of companies with market entries in each major product class. Of 45 major firms, 38 have entries in the largest market, and 14 have entries in the smallest market.

New Product Entries

Despite increasing expenditures and the fact that approximately 14 percent of all employees are engaged in research and development, the number of single-entity new product discoveries is declining. Mitchell has observed that there is general agreement that the number of new single chemical entities introduced on the market has declined since the 1962 amendments to the Food, Drug, and Cosmetic Act.[13] Martin Baily found that the research and development expenditures required to introduce a new chemical entity doubled since the 1962 drug amendments. He concluded that introduction of new chemical entities is a function of: (1) past research and development; (2) the "tightness of FDA regulations"; and (3) the depletion of available new product development opportunities.[14] Whatever the cause, pharmaceutical single-entity new product innovation has decreased during the past 15 years, according to Paul de Haen.[15]

[11]Douglas L. Cocks, "Product Innovation and Dynamic Elements of Competition in the Ethical Pharmaceutical Industry," *Drug Development and Marketing*, ed. Robert B. Helms (Washington, D.C.: American Enterprise Institute for Public Policy Research, 1975), pp. 225-254.

[12]Stephen Hymer and Peter Pashigian, "Turnover of Firms as a Measure of Market Behavior," *Review of Economics and Statistics* (February, 1962), pp. 82-87.

[13]Samuel A. Mitchell, "Regulation and Innovation: Outlook and Impact," *Research From Washington Reports*, Note-31-75 (Washington, D. C.: Research from Washington, August 5, 1975), p. 1.

[14]Martin N. Baily, "Research and Development Costs and Returns: The U.S. Pharmaceutical Industry," *Journal of Political Economy* (January/February, 1972).

[15]Paul de Haen, *New Products Parade: 1973-1974* (New York: Paul de Haen, Inc., February, 1975).

Table 2.

Firm	Number of Therapeutic Categories in Which Firm Had Sales	Ratio of the Number of Therapeutic Categories in Which Firm Had Sales to the Total Number of Categories	(%) Market Share
Lilly	43	.876	7.9%
Hoffmann-La Roche	21	.429	7.5
American Home Products	39	.796	6.6
Merck	38	.776	6.0
Bristol-Myers	21	.429	4.2
Abbott	36	.735	3.7
Pfizer	27	.551	3.6
Ciba-Geigy	27	.551	3.6
Upjohn	33	.673	3.5
Squibb	29	.592	3.4
Smith-Kline	25	.510	3.3
Johnson & Johnson	29	.592	2.7
Schering-Plough	24	.490	2.7
Parke-Davis	41	.837	2.7
Searle	15	.306	2.5
Lederle	26	.531	2.3
Sandoz-Wander	27	.551	2.0
Robins	25	.510	2.0
Sterling	35	.714	1.9
Burroughs-Wellcome	27	.551	1.8
Warner-Lambert	25	.510	1.7

SOURCE: Douglas L. Cocks, "Product Innovation and the Dynamic Elements of Competition in the Ethical Pharmaceutical Industry," *Drug Development and Marketing*, ed. Robert B. Helms (Washington, D.C.: American Enterprise Institute for Public Policy Research, 1975), compiled from sources and tables, pp. 237-241.

For each new chemical-entity product, about two duplicate chemical-entity products are introduced.[16] It seems that efforts by more than one firm often are required to gain widespread knowledge, trial, and acceptance of new products.

The decline in single-entity new product introductions is having a profound effect on marketing activities. The most pronounced effects might be: (1) a greater tendency to promote existing pharmacological entities; (2) proliferation of brands of the same entity, that is, introduction of a large number of duplicate products; (3) a reduction in marketing expenses necessitating more efficiency in conveying information; (4) greater emphasis on "information content" messages in promotion rather than "novelty" messages; (5) increasing ratio of refills to new prescriptions, thus utilizing information on long-term drug use; (6) more emphasis on price competition and added promotion

[16] *Ibid.*

Table 3. Domestic Sales and Number of Marketers of Ethical Drugs by Product Class, 1974

	Sales (millions)	Number of Companies Indicating Sales (major 45 firms)
Central nervous system	$1,395.9	38
Anti-infectives	834.3	31
Neoplasms and endocrine	531.3	27
Digestives and genitourinary	519.9	38
Cardiovasculars	479.6	31
Vitamins and nutrients	457.4	32
Respiratory system	335.9	33
Dermatologicals	178.5	30
Biologicals	141.5	13
Diagnostic agents	113.5	14
Other	273.0	23
TOTAL	$5,260.8	45

SOURCE: Pharmaceutical Manufacturers Association, *Annual Survey Report: 1974-1975* (Washington, D. C.: PMA, 1975), p. 7.

of generic products; and (7) more importance attached to service and non-product elements of the marketing mix.

Product line decisions are among the most critical to the long-run growth, stability, and success of any firm. The firm's product portfolio determines the particular physician specialties that the firm potentially may satisfy and provides a financial return to be used for research and development. At all times the firm must weigh the profit potential against the risks of doing business.

The decline in new single-entity product innovation has necessarily increased the life of existing chemical entities but not necessarily brands. The implications of a shift of many firms' product portfolios from a balance of products across all stages of the life cycle (introduction, growth, maturity, and decline stages) to a concentration in the maturity stage are apparent. Because of the decline in new chemical entities, many firms' portfolios are now stacked with products approaching maturity stages. Highest profitability can be expected during the last parts of the growth stage and the early maturity stage. Successful products in these stages provide the needed funds for research and development. Once these periods pass, however, profits dwindle because of pricing and other competitive factors.

Legal restraints affect all levels of product management. Pharmaceutical manufacturers are required by law to provide substantial evidence that the drug is effective and safe for its intended uses. This requirement has lengthened the delay between discovery and introduction and has diminished the number of new products marketed each year. Also, it has substantially increased the costs of bringing a new drug to the market and has increased research expenditures and activities generally. On the benefit side, FDA requirements have imposed upon drug manufacturers more systemized planning and operational activities and have enhanced their perceived responsibility, resulting in greater self-scrutiny and self-regulation and longer-range market planning.

MARKETING PROMOTIONAL COSTS

Specific promotional activities are a function of market opportunity, communication techniques, and governmental regulation. The role of promotion in the pharmaceutical industry, and particularly specific forms, is poorly understood by many individuals. C. Joseph Stetler, president of the Pharmaceutical Manufacturers Association, has said:

> The amount of money and effort directed toward the promotion of prescription drugs to physicians, and the place of that promotion in the process by which prescribing decisions are made, comprise two of the least understood facets of our operations.[17]

How costly is pharmaceutical promotion, and what are its functions?

During 1973, it was estimated that total promotional costs for ethical drugs in the United States amounted to $767,500,000 and were allocated as follows: sales representatives' time, $435 million; sales representatives' literature, $34.5 million; journal advertising, $83 million; direct mail advertising, $54 million; sampling, $92 million; and conventions, exhibits, and miscellaneous, $69 million.[18]

The cost of industry marketing is inherently high because of the large amount of documentation — regulatory and medical — needed to explain the products; and because of the relatively high technological exchange of information, including a good deal of individualized service to the physician.

Marketing-cost ratios (that is, the total expenditures on behalf of marketing expressed as a percentage of net sales in the same period) are calculated by most manufacturing concerns in an attempt to determine the appropriateness of investment outlay for the marketing functions which, of

---

[17]C. Joseph Stetler, "Statement of the Pharmaceutical Manufacturers Association to the National Council of Churches of Christ in the U.S.A.—Subcommittee on Drug Advertising" (November, 1972), p. 18.

[18]FDC Reports, Inc., "The Pink Sheet," *FDC Reports* (Washington, D.C.: FDC Reports, Inc., August 20, 1973).

Table 4. Average Ratio of Marketing Costs to Net Sales Prescription Drug Products

Total costs	27.0%
Marketing support costs	11.2
Selling related costs	15.8

SOURCE: Abstracted from The Conference Board, *Marketing-Cost Ratios of U.S. Manufacturers* (New York: The Conference Board, 1975).

course, help to generate sales income. A significant overinvestment or underinvestment might retard the firm's sales and profit potential. However, it is quite the norm for competing marketers to have highly dissimilar ratios, even when neglecting to consider the extreme cases. For example, based on a census of the industry, the Pharmaceutical Manufacturers Association reports that for the entire industry the average ratio of marketing costs to net sales is about 14 percent, while the Conference Board reports a ratio of 27 percent for a sample of its members (see Table 4).[19] As partial explanation, the latter includes two cost items not computed by the former—marketing research, and marketing administration and planning.*

Manufacturers' marketing-cost ratios offer one possible basis for comparison of their marketing activities, even though this has no necessary relation to ultimate profits obtained. The Conference Board undertook several phases of research from 1971 to 1975, and the following material has been abstracted from their analysis, *Marketing-Cost Ratios of U.S. Manufacturers* (1975):

> Research confirms that certain distinguishing features of manufacturers' products, marketing operations, selling practices and distribution methods are correlated—some positively, some negatively—with the ratio of their total marketing costs to their sales. And this substantially reduces the variance in cost ratios which remains to be explained in other ways; e.g., by differences in the marketing productivity of different marketers.[20]

The Conference Board found that ethical pharmaceuticals are highly

---

[19]The 14 percent marketing cost to sales ratio was calculated by dividing the $768 million marketing expense figure reported by FDC Reports, Inc., "The Pink Sheet"' *FDC Reports* (Washington, D. C.: FDC Reports, Inc., August 20, 1973), by the $5,507 million sales figure reported by the PMA. PMA reports that the sales figure is only for human-use pharmaceuticals in finished form [Pharmaceuticals Manufacturers Association, *Annual Survey Report: 1973–1974* (Washington, D.C.: PMA, December, 1974)].

*The Conference Board reports marketing cost ratios for most major U.S. industries. It cannot be concluded that these ratios represent the total industry, but they do represent some subset of firms and products of the industry.

[20]The Conference Board, *Marketing Cost Ratios of U.S. Manufacturers* (New York: The Conference Board, Inc., 1975).

"marketing-intensive." One should not conclude that product class differences cause variations in marketing costs. Other factors, five of which are listed below, seem significantly related to differences in the total marketing-cost ratios.[21]

1. The frequency with which the product is purchased can be a factor. With many pharmaceuticals the frequency of purchase may be low, given the amount of personal contact required by the selling firm.

2. There may be an apparent loss of efficiency when the size of the selling organization is required to be large in order to service many geographically dispersed prescribers.

3. A look at sales volume of the individual product line, compared with others in its product class, indicates a beneficial influence of high market share upon the marketing-cost ratio. While the pharmaceutical industry does have some products with a high share of the market for a particular pharmacological entity, no manufacturer commands a strong share of any doctor's total prescribing. Physicians prescribe on a product/disease indication basis.

4. Another factor is the number of drug distribution and dispensing points. For example, in the controlled substances area alone, as of January 1976, there were 524,734 registrants authorized by the Drug Enforcement Administration to possess or distribute controlled drugs.[22] Thus, a relatively decentralized distribution effort must be supported.

5. The size of the geographic market area within which the product is sold is also a factor. National distribution to both urban and rural areas is more costly than selective distribution and marketing to only highly concentrated areas.

As Table 5 shows, manufacturer expenditures and profit represent only 46 percent of the cost of sales to the consumer; the remainder is for wholesaling and retailing. The ratio of manufacturers' marketing, management, and distribution costs to retail sales is about 15 percent.

Constraints on Pharmaceutical Marketing Promotion

A presentation of salient legal restrictions on pharmaceutical promotion can isolate the boundaries of each promotional activity.

[21]These five factors were among those listed by The Conference Board, *ibid.* This author made the specific comments regarding the pharmaceutical industry.

[22]International Narcotic Enforcement Officers Association, "News: U.S. Department of Justice, Drug Enforcement Administration,"*International Drug Report,* Vol. 17, No. 10 (New York: International Narcotic Enforcement Officers Association, October, 1976), p. 6.

Table 5. Expenses and Earnings in the Sales of Retail Products, Manufacturers Only

	Ratio to Retail Sales	Ratio to Own Sales
Production expenses	.15	.33
Research and development costs	.05	.11
Other expenses (marketing, management, and distribution)	.15	.33
U.S. income taxes	.06	.12
Earnings	.05	.11
Percentage of total	.46	1.00

SOURCE: Pharmaceutical Manufacturers Association, *Prescription Drug Industry Fact Book: 1973* (Washington, D.C.: PMA, 1973), p. 32.

Pharmaceutical marketing must be highly sensitive to social pressure and interests. Social environmental pressures surrounding the drug industry have created a sense of "self-regulation" within many firms, witnessed by the current extent of planning, monitoring, analyzing, specifying, and controlling marketing activities. The pharmaceutical firm is faced with social concern regarding its pricing and profit-making potential. This concern perhaps is based on a lack of information. In essence, public skepticism revolves around the inelasticity of the demand curve for pharmaceuticals at particular times. Physicians may be less price sensitive than consumers, since the patient pays for the drug. In addition, physicians, when evaluating drugs, process a great deal of medical information about drugs and have relatively little time to analyze cost/treatment benefits. Public pressures, along with catalytic political sentiment, have stimulated greatly the growth of the government's role as "regulator," despite concern over governmental intervention into the private practice of medicine.

Law requires that all promotion communicate a balanced view of the drug's potential—pros and cons, precautions, warnings, side effects, indications, contraindications, and so forth—in order that the prescribing physician has as much relevant knowledge as is possible on which to base an informed decision. These regulations take effect once the product has been approved and cover all advertisements and other descriptive printed matter issued or caused to be issued by the manufacturers, packers, or distributors.

Governmental regulations have imposed the following requirements on advertising and labeling:

1. The established name (that is, the generic name) should be printed in letters at least half as large as the proprietary name and should accompany the proprietary name each time that it is featured.

2. A brief summary of side effects, contraindications, and effectiveness should be included in any advertisements that purport to give any representation or suggestion relating to a drug.

3. Fair balance must be maintained in presenting relevant positive and negative information on a drug.

4. Recommendations or suggested uses in advertisements must be confined to those contained in labeling and permitted by the FDA in appropriate new drug applications.[23]

With these legal requirements and other constraints in mind, it is appropriate to discuss the individual promotional activities engaged in by pharmaceutical firms.

Sales Activities

Approximately 20,000 sales representatives are employed to call on physicians, pharmacists, dentists, wholesalers, and hospitals. The cost is about $435 million,[24] or 40 cents per prescription.[25] The firm with the largest sales force has about one salesperson for each 300 physicians. Most firms have substantially fewer.

It is estimated that about 60 percent of the total marketing expenses are allocated to the activities of manufacturers' representatives. Although this cost has been gradually increasing in current dollars, inflation has accounted for all of that increase. As Table 6 shows, in real dollars the cost of sales

Table 6. Marketing Expenditure Trends, 1970-1975 (Index of Real Dollars)

Year	Sales Representatives	Journal Ads	Direct Mail	Total
1970	100.0	100.0	100.0	100.0
1971	100.1	94.7	84.5	96.8
1972	102.1	90.7	79.4	96.9
1973	104.4	94.0	77.4	99.2
1974	97.3	88.6	68.6	92.4
1975	90.3	82.3	67.0	86.0

SOURCE: IMS America, Ambler, Pennsylvania. Current dollar expenditures were deflated by the GNP implicit price deflator.

[23]U.S., Office of the Federal Register, National Archives and Records Service, General Services Administration, "Food and Drugs," *Code of Federal Regulations*, Vol. 21, Parts 201-202 (Washington, D.C.: U.S. Government Printing Office, 1975).

[24]FDC Reports, Inc., *loc. cit.*

[25]*Ibid.*

representatives has declined in the last couple of years. The 1975 level of expenditures was about 10 percent below the 1970 figure.

In general, when the product is complex, the more effective sales presentation relies on a strategy based on technical information rather than nontechnical persuasion. Pharmaceutical salespeople stimulate sales by communicating important information to physicians.

A pharmaceutical company's medical sales representatives are an important part of its information program. These individuals receive continuous in-house training in pharmacology and other medical aspects of drug use so that they may convey up-to-date information to physicians, hospital personnel, pharmacists, and other health professionals. The sales representative has the responsibility to promote to medical professionals in a manner which will encourage the appropriate use of pharmaceutical and other health care products and services. To accomplish this task, sales representatives must understand selected therapeutic treatment goals, the complexities of patient management, product distribution, and applicable federal and state regulations regarding labeling and distribution of pharmaceuticals. More importantly, they should have a thorough technical understanding of the advantages and limitations of each product or service before calling on a physician.

The advisory nature of the sales message and the exchange of technical information afford a two-way communication flow, by personal contact, which is more instructive than the one-way promotion characteristic of much retail marketing. The sales representative serves several functions for both the physician and the firm, among which are the following:

1. A source of information on drug products. The sales representative is able to convey to the physician information on new drugs and new information on old drugs.

2. A conduit to the expertise available to the physician through the professional staff of the pharmaceutical firm. The sales person communicates messages to the physician from the experts within the pharmaceutical company. In doing so he can answer questions of a limited scope or convey specific information requested by the physician.

3. A messenger of information from the physician to others in the firm. This affords the firm sensitivity towards its customers, provides on-the-spot information concerning possible adverse reactions with drugs, better forecasting and, therefore, product efficiency.

4. A problem solver in the drug distribution system. The sales person can help monitor inventory levels, sometimes make deliveries, and maintain surveillance of the appropriate distribution of pharmaceuticals.

5. A forum to discuss with the physician therapeutic alternatives and patient

management problems. The sales person will discuss those of his products he believes have the potential to fill this need for the physician.

Direct Mail

The use of direct mail promotion has been relatively stable in recent years and now represents less than 10 percent of total promotion expenses. The number of mailings has declined, and at the same time the total cost of such distribution also has declined sharply (see Table 6).

Direct mail has the advantage of being targeted directly to an individual in much the same manner as sales visits. Because a specific audience is sought, direct mail tends to carry more elaborate information than other forms of printed advertising. More voluminous and technical data requiring, for example, charts and graphs can be economically mailed, whereas such information would be prohibitively expensive to communicate to the prescriber through other printed promotional sources.

Journal Advertising

Like other marketing expenditure items, according to an industry source, journal advertising in constant dollars has also been declining in recent years (see Table 6).

Journal advertising is another vehicle for communicating information to physicians. It may be used to reinforce the information already communicated to physicians by the sales representative or through other means.[26] Most marketing executives do not think in terms of one advertisement but of integrative advertising campaigns. A campaign would be a series of ads with a common theme or objective intended to have synergistic effects. The objectives of the campaign might range from introducing a new product (but not attempting to obtain trial) to reminding physicians of the actions of existing products. Whether a single advertising campaign is successful is extremely difficult to measure, since it is seldom undertaken in the absence of other marketing activities. Most research on advertisements in pharmaceutical journals indicates that they rarely produce the final decision to use or not use a product; rather, they inform, remind, and stimulate. As a side benefit, journal advertising, like other forms of pharmaceutical promotion, might prevent inappropriate prescribing, since the FDA, in general, requires full disclosure of side effects and other cautionary information.

[26]E. F. Linder, "Medical Advertising—Its Role, Ethics and Concepts," *New York State Journal of Medicine*, Vol. 64 (1964), 1990.

In drug advertising, there often is need to deliver a complicated and important message to informed and unusually sophisticated users—including data on uses, contraindications, side effects, formulations, and dosage.

Rather than creating a demand for a product, journal advertising is geared to inform and remind the physician concerning the wide range of product use. Journal advertising also facilitates entry into the market for new and improved products,[27] which compete with products that previously may have achieved wide acceptance by the medical profession. Aside from direct scientific substantiation, advertising in medical journals includes extensive summaries of product information from required FDA labeling and package insert materials.

Sampling

Pharmaceutical samples to physicians may permit informal clinical evaluation of the product to help assess its value to the individual physician's practice. They also may allow evaluation on a patient-specific basis to determine his or her response and tolerance and provide the patient with a convenient means to begin treatment immediately. In some cases they are used to assist low-income patients.[28]

Today sampling has increased to a level equal to expenditures for journal advertising. Some pharmaceutical firms and physicians voice problems with sampling practices. The greatest difficulty appears to be inefficient distribution, when some doctors receive samples wholly inappropriate for their patients. The result is either the return of the unused product or its disposal, both of which are wasteful. There is also some question whether the practicing physician obtains systematic feedback from patients using samples.

Pricing

Pricing policies in the pharmaceutical industry are complex[29] and affect a firm's profitability. Uncertainty in demand makes it difficult to calculate a marginal revenue for a product. Pricing also affects the marketing effort. While no set formula exists for pricing pharmaceuticals, the following factors

[27]Lester G. Telser, William Best, John Egan, Harlow N. Higgin Gotham, "The Theory of Supply with Applications to the Ethical Pharmaceutical Industry," *The Journal of Law and Economics* (October, 1975), p. 477.

[28]Market Measures, Inc., "New Methods of Sampling Pharmaceuticals," paper presented at the Medical Marketing Conference, 1972.

[29]For a review of pricing in pharmaceuticals, see J. D. McEvilla, "Price Determination Theory in the Pharmaceutical Industry,"*Drug and Cosmetic Industry*, Vol. 82 (1958), p. 34.

are often considered before establishing a price: research and development costs, both historical and projected future expenditures; marketing, selling, and support costs; production, materials, and distribution costs; the prices of competing and substitute products; and the average daily cost of therapy to the patient.

In the introductory stage, prices must be high enough to cover investment costs, assuming relatively uncertain life cycles. Also, the firm attempts to price its products to cover expenses incurred for drugs that do not reach the market and R&D efforts that fail to yield a commercial product. The nature of research is such that marketable discoveries do not often occur, nor are they easily predictable.

A great deal of public debate has centered on the issue of generic drug pricing. Some differences between marketing generic products and branded products are discussed briefly below.

The price differences between generic and branded products are sometimes large. The most commonly cited reasons are that brand drug prices must bear the cost of all new and old research and development and that brand drugs have more costly and better quality control. Also, brand products support the costs of introducing new products. The expense of informing physicians is substantial. Early stages in a product life cycle require an extensive information dispersion campaign. This includes designing and paying for pertinent clinical patient studies and preparing and communicating technical information about the product. New product introductions, made almost entirely by research-intensive firms, are probably the most risky and expensive marketing and production ventures. Failure at this level can be devastating. Trade name drugs must be priced to support the full range of services offered to the medical profession and the consumer by the pharmaceutical industry.

From a marketing point of view, competing only on the basis of low price generally can be viable over the long run only for the marginal producer. This is true because value and prices are not directly equated: Value comes not in buying the product but in consuming it. A major factor in determining the value of its consumption is how well the product is prescribed. Appropriate prescribing can only occur when nonprice, as well as price, information is available. Typically, the marginal producers are dependent on the research-intensive firms' product promotion to pave the way for physician acceptance of the drug. They are also dependent on producers of trade name drugs to develop all the technical and clinical support for the drug. In the absence of brand drugs, the generic producers would be required to perform the functions traditionally borne by brand name manufacturers. Their marketing costs would then increase and, consequently, force an increase in prices to the consumer.

Distribution

Distribution of pharmaceuticals is achieved primarily in two ways: *direct* (from manufacturer to retailer to consumer) and *indirect* (from manufacturer to wholesaler to retailer to consumer). Indirect distribution is the traditional method. In addition to wholesalers and retailers, other distributors of prescription drugs include private and government hospitals and clinics. Table 7 indicates the relative percentage of drugs moving through each channel.

Wholesalers continue to be the largest single conduit for drug distribution. The manufacturer benefits from an indirect distribution strategy because several functions necessary to doing business are shifted from the manufacturer to the wholesaler. The process of efficient distribution requires not only cost efficiency but also certainty in delivery. In some cases the wholesaler may be less concerned about a single drug than its manufacturer would like, and the manufacturer's reputation can be damanged. While the manufacturer gains leverage by using middlemen, he can lose some control over the delivery of his product.

Retailers can be divided into private or chain pharmacies. Pharmacists have extensive contact with patients and limited contact with physicians. As such, they affect the absolute use and volume of a particular brand. When

Table 7. Manufacturers' Direct Dosage Form Sales in United States, 1974[a]

	Value (millions)	Total Market Share	Percentage Change in Dollar Volume (1973-1974)
Wholesalers	$2,747.8	45.2%	+ 11.2%
Retailers	1,709.6	28.1	+ 4.8
Private hospitals	951.3	15.6	+17.6
State and local government hospitals	292.5	4.8	+ 8.8
Federal government hospitals	156.4	2.6	+ 2.1
Practitioners (private, medical and dental)	90.4	1.5	+20.0
Other federal government	75.5	1.2	+17.1
Manufacturers, repackagers, and all others	59.0	1.0	—
TOTAL	$6,082.5	100.0%	+10.4%

[a] Direct dosage form as opposed to bulk dosage form.

SOURCE: Pharmaceutical Manufacturers Association, *Annual Survey Report: 1974-1975* (Washington, D. C.: PMA, December, 1975), p. 6.

the manufacturer markets through wholesalers, he often risks losing control of the messages that are communicated to pharmacists. Pharmacists are in a position to promote a particular brand to a patient when the prescription is generically written or to a doctor on those occasions when he asks the pharmacist for advice. Generic substitution laws are increasing the pharmacist's prescription-filling discretion. Consequently, manufacturers are becoming more sensitive to the pharmacist and his needs, and some of the sales activities traditionally reserved for the physician are being reallocated to the pharmacist.[30]

CONCLUSIONS

The pharmaceutical manufacturer's marketing mix, including products, promotion, pricing, and distribution, offers a broad range of competitive options. Overall changes are evolutionary rather than revolutionary. However, several trends in pharmaceutical marketing have emerged recently, and the possibility of significant changes in the near future is apparent. Many future practices will be in response to technological changes in drug treatment, legislation affecting prescribing, a greater role of the pharmacist, new marketing tools and techniques, and intensified competition. Several implications follow:

1. Greater reliance on marketing research and marketing information systems in allocating marketing resources.
2. More emphasis on promotional efforts to pharmacists, including specialized print and promotion for this group.
3. Greater use of electronic media in promotion to physicians in order to support the sales representative in communicating specialized information.
4. Increased competition in established product classes due to patent expirations.
5. More emphasis on total health systems, including integrated computer technologies for diagnosis as well as treatment. Drugs will be integral parts of total diagnosis and treatment systems rather than isolated entities.
6. More specialized marketing personnel in behavioral sciences and statistical sciences.
7. Greater marketing inputs for research and development planning to better match market needs with research opportunities.

[30]Gilbert D. Harrell and Donald S. Henley, "Pharmacy Marketing in a Changing Environment" (in review).

Since in real terms marketing expenditures are declining, most of the trends are toward better and more efficient marketing approaches rather than increased expenditures. The pharmaceutical marketing community is likely to be better educated, including advanced degree talents at the undergraduate, master's, and even doctorate levels. Interdisciplinary skills will be used more in the future than in the past. The total impact of these potential changes will be a low-profile pharmaceutical marketing approach that is more sensitive to the needs of the U.S. health care system. Consequently, the use and distribution of prescription products are likely to be affected in a positive way.

5

The Changing
Pharmaceutical Research
and Development Environment

Jerome E. Schnee

Associate Professor
Graduate School of Business Administration
Rutgers University

Erol Caglarcan

Political Economist
Hoffmann-La Roche Inc.

INTRODUCTION

Technological change in the American ethical pharmaceutical industry has become a subject of considerable interest to economists, drug industry executives, and public policy decision-makers during the last decade. Considerable attention has been focused on the declining rate of pharmaceutical innovation; the changing costs, risks, and profitability of pharmaceutical innovation; the transfer of pharmaceutical technology between organizations and between countries; and the economic costs and benefits of the 1962 amendments to the federal Food and Drug Act. This chapter will review some major dimensions of the changing research environment in the pharmaceutical industry.

The primary purpose of pharmaceutical research is to aid in the prevention, diagnosis, and treatment of disease and general promotion of health. The pharmaceutical industry research effort achieves these goals through the introduction of new therapies. In this effort pharmaceutical firms compete vigorously. This intense new-product competition originated with the introduction of penicillin and streptomycin in the mid-1940s.

Thus, drug research, as we know it today, is actually a fairly recent phenomenon. It has been estimated that, measured in terms of man-year effort, more than 95 percent of all pharmaceutical research carried out since the dawn of history has occurred since 1935.[1] The U.S. ethical pharmaceutical industry annually spends over $1 billion for research and development, a twentyfold increase over the last 25 years.

One significant feature of pharmaceutical R&D is the high proportion that is financed by the companies themselves. In 1976, less than 1 percent of the pharmaceutical industry's R&D funds were provided by the government as compared to 42 percent for American industry in general.[2] The R&D expenditures of U.S. pharmaceutical manufacturers amount to about 11 percent of the industry's net sales, a figure five times greater than the 2 percent level for U.S. industry as a whole. The industry also ranks first in the proportion of its R&D funds allocated to basic research.

The pharmaceutical industry's R&D expenditures are distributed among a wide range of firms of various sizes. Of 70 pharmaceutical companies reporting R&D programs in 1973, 78 percent each invested more than $1 million in R&D activities; and 40 percent each spent $10 million or more. The number of firms with research budgets above $20 million increased from 8 to 19 between 1968 and 1977.[3]

However, not all the firms have been able to stay in this research race. Although product discovery and development are now essential to the survival and growth of individual pharmaceutical firms, some companies have been unable to introduce significant new products on a regular basis. Consequently, they have suffered erosion of market positions with corresponding declines in profits. The shifting fortunes of Carter-Wallace illustrate this phenomenon. The firm became extremely profitable after it introduced Miltown, the "first" tranquilizer, in 1955. The introduction of Librium and Valium by Hoffmann-La Roche in the early 1960s and Carter-Wallace's inability to develop significant new drugs caused sharp declines in the company's profitability.[4]

[1]Max Tischler and R. G. Denkewalter, "Drug Research—Whence and Whither," *Progress in Drug Research,* ed. by Ernest Jucker (Basel, Switzerland, 1966), p. 12.

[2]Pharmaceutical Manufacturers Association, *Annual Survey Report, Ethical Pharmaceutical Industry Operations, 1975–1976* (Washington, D.C.: PMA, 1976).

[3]*Ibid.*

[4]Miltown, which was introduced in 1955, was Carter-Wallace's first profitable ethical drug. The product immediately became remarkably popular and extremely profitable. Thus, Carter's overall net profits jumped by 43 percent in 1955, by 100 percent in 1956, and by 125 percent in 1957. Overall net sales climbed by 56 percent in 1956 and 83 percent in 1957. Librium was introduced in 1960 and quickly began cutting into Carter's market. For the year ending March, 1961, Carter's overall net sales and profits declined by 4 percent and 16 percent, respectively. The impact continued with the introduction of Valium in 1963. In six of the ten fiscal years since Valium's appearance on the market, Carter's overall net profits have declined, hitting a low point of −23.5 percent for the year ended March, 1973.

THE RATE OF PHARMACEUTICAL INNOVATION

The rate of pharmaceutical innovation reached its peak between 1951 and 1960 as the accelerated growth of R&D spending resulted in an increasing flow of new products. During the 1950s, 3563 new products and dosage forms were introduced into the U.S. pharmaceutical market. New drugs can be classified into the following four categories: (1) new chemical entities; (2) duplicate products; (3) compounded products; and (4) alternate dosage forms.[5]

New chemical entities are unique, new products and those which achieve the greatest degree of chemical differentiation. About 12 percent of the 3563 products introduced during the 1951-1960 period were new entities (Table 1). Both the volume of all new products and new chemical entities declined during the 1960s. The annual average number of new products and new chemicals introduced between 1961 and 1970 was 139 and 20, respectively, as compared to 356 and 43, respectively, during the 1950s. The rate of innovation remained considerably below the 1951-60 average through the early 1970s (Table 1).[6]

The decline in the rate of pharmaceutical innovation has been further analyzed by Dr. Barry Bloom, an industry research executive. Using a more restrictive definition of innovation, he analyzed the rate of introduction of basic new agents for six five-year periods from 1941 through August 1970 (Table 2).[7] The rate of innovation reached a maximum in the last half of the 1950s when the annual average of basic new agents reached almost 40. The rate was approximately halved during the 1961-65 period in comparison to the previous period. The rate further declined by almost half again, in the 1966-70 period, reaching a low of 12.

Bloom also found an uneven decline in the rate of basic new agent in-

[5]New drug products are classified into these four categories by Paul de Haen in his annual *New Product Surveys* using the following definitions: (1) *New Chemical Entity* indicates products that are new, single-chemical entities not previously known, including new salts; (2) *Duplicate single products*, products such as dexamethasone or griseofulvin which are put out by various manufacturers; (3) *Compounded products*, any products having more than one active ingredient; (4) *Alternate dosage forms*, products previously marketed in tablets and now offered in ampules, capsules, liquid, etc.

[6]Paul de Haen, *Non-Proprietary Name Index*, Vol. XX (New York: Paul de Haen, Inc., 1973).

[7]A drug product was included in Bloom's edited list only if it was, at the time of market introduction, a new single-chemical entity intended for human therapeutic use, that did not fall into any of the following excluded categories: biologicals such as vaccines; diagnostic aids; hospital solutions; nonabsorbed high molecular weight compounds; impure extracts of natural origin; new uses and/or formulations of previously marketed drugs; new single components included in previously marketed mixtures; and new salts of previously marketed drugs. Although Bloom excludes new salts, his edited list does include new esters and other covalently bonded derivatives of previously marketed drugs. See Barry M. Bloom, "The Rate of Contemporary Drug Discovery," *Lex et Scientia*, Vol. 8, No. 1 (January-March, 1971).

Table 1. New Product Introductions in the Ethical Pharmaceutical Industry, 1950-1974

Year	Total New Products	New Single Chemicals	Duplicate Products	Compounded Products	New Dosage Forms
1950	326	28	100	198	118
1951	321	35	74	212	120
1952	314	35	77	202	170
1953	353	48	79	226	97
1954	380	38	87	255	108
1955	403	31	90	282	96
1956	401	42	79	280	66
1957	400	51	88	261	96
1958	370	44	73	253	109
1959	315	63	49	203	104
1960	306	45	62	199	98
1961	260	39	32	189	106
1962	250	27	43	180	84
1963	199	16	34	149	52
1964	157	17	29	111	41
1965	112	23	18	71	22
1966	80	12	15	53	26
1967	82	25	25	32	14
1968	87	11	26	50	21
1969	62	9	22	31	12
1970	105	16	50	39	23
1971	83	14	40	29	30
1972	64	11	35	18	30
1973	74	19	37	18	17
1974	83	18	42	23	26
Total	5587	717	1306	3564	1686

SOURCE: Paul de Haen, *Ten Year New Product Survey, 1950-1960; Non-Proprietary Name Index*, Vol. VI (New York: Paul de Haen, Inc., 1967); *New Products Parade, 1973-1974* (New York: Paul de Haen, Inc., 1975).

Table 2. Basic New Pharmaceutical Agents

Five-Year Periods	Average Number of Basic New Agents Introduced Per Year
1941-45	10
1946-50	18
1951-55	31
1956-60	39
1961-65	20
1966-70 (through August)	12

SOURCE: Barry M. Bloom, "The Rate of Contemporary Drug Discovery," *Lex et Scientia*, Vol. 8, No. 1 (January-March, 1971).

troductions among product categories when he compared introductions for the five-year period immediately preceding (1958-62) and following (1963-67) the 1962 amendments to the federal Food and Drug Act. In well-established drug categories where a number of useful agents already existed (antihistamines, antispasmodics, corticosteroids), few, if any, new agents were introduced. The drop in psychotherapeutic drugs was not as pronounced. The negligible decline in antibiotics was attributed to some important technical breakthroughs in the penicillin and cephalosporin fields in the years before the 1963-67 period.

The largest number of innovations between 1963 and 1967 was in cancer chemotherapy; this is viewed as the cumulative effect of a joint effort on the part of government, universities, and the pharmaceutical industry to curb cancer. Also, because cancer drugs tend to have a narrow range of usefulness, a relatively large number of them get developed.

The decline in the rate of pharmaceutical innovation has generated considerable controversy. Industry critics cite the relatively small number of new products as evidence that the industry is becoming more inefficient. Industry spokesmen dispute these contentions and attribute the change in research productivity to the impact of new federal drug regulations.

It appears that the explanation is somewhat more complicated than either of these views. The two decades following World War II saw the rapid development of numerous significant new drugs, largely because of substantial advances in the biomedical sciences. However, future advances in drug research are likely to be more difficult. Although medicinal chemistry has made great strides in discovering methods for synthesizing complicated molecules, and isolating and identifying active substances from plants, bacteria, and mammals, the output of biological knowledge has failed to keep pace. To be sure, we know more about biomedical processes today than ever before. However, as new biomedical frontiers are opened up, we are faced with larger areas of the unknown. The views of Dr. John Burns are instructive in this regard:

> We lack basic knowledge of drug action and of disease processes in man, and this lack is certain to delay future advances, especially in treating diseases such as cancer, congenital disease, and viral infections. Even when new drugs are developed, their introduction is often delayed because medical opinions differ on what constitutes valid safety and efficacy data. In short, we are confronted by a widening biological knowledge gap.[8]

---

[8]Pharmaceutical Manufacturers Association, "Symposium on Progress in Drug Research" (Washington, D. C.: PMA, 1969), as discussed in J. Burns, "Modern Drug Research," The American University, *Proceedings of the First Seminar on Economics of Pharmaceutical Innovation* (1969), 56-57.

THE CHANGING COSTS, RISKS, AND PROFITABILITY
OF PHARMACEUTICAL R&D

The declining rate of pharmaceutical innovation during the last decade has been accompanied by sharp increases in the cost, duration, and risk of new product development. The magnitude of these changes is suggested by comparing estimates of these development parameters for the early 1970s with comparable estimates for the pre-1962 period.

In 1971 Harold Clymer, an industry research executive, estimated that it cost his firm an average of $3 to $5 million to develop a new chemical entity. The average development time was estimated at five to seven years. Clymer estimated that only one out of ten new chemical entity development projects resulted in a marketed product. The cost of this one marketed product approximated $12 million ($3.5 million for the one marketed product and a total expenditure of $8.5 million for the nine unsuccessful products).[9]

One of the authors has provided estimates for the pre-1962 period in a study of the development project portfolio of one large pharmaceutical firm. Data were collected for the 134 development projects conducted by the firm between 1950 and 1967. Of the 75 successful projects studied by Schnee, most were completed before 1962; only three projects were completed between 1962 and 1967. The average development cost and duration for the 17 new chemical entities in the Schnee sample are considerably lower than Clymer's 1971 estimates ($.5 million compared with $3 to $5 million, and two years as opposed to five to seven years).[10]

Development project attrition rates and the resulting costs of developing a marketed product have changed even more dramatically. Current project attrition rates (90 percent of development projects fail) are much higher than those in the Schnee study (63 per cent of development projects failed). As a result, Clymer's estimated development cost for one marketed product ($12 million) is more than ten times greater than the comparable figure for the pre-1962 period ($1.1 million).

These huge increases in the costs and length of drug R&D and the accompanying decline in new product introductions have combined to sharply reduce the rate of return on R&D investment. Clymer's 1971 estimates of

[9]Harold A. Clymer, "The Economics of Drug Innovation," *The Development and Control of New Drug Products*, eds. M. Pernarowski and M. Darrach (Vancouver: University of British Columbia, 1972).

[10]Jerome Schnee, "Development Costs: Determinants and Overruns," *Journal of Business* (July, 1972). A recent University of Rochester study estimated that the *research and development* of a new pharmaceutical product averaged 10 to 13 years and cost $55 million in 1976 dollars. See Ronald Hansen, "Comments on the Proposed Changes in FDA's Trade Secrets Policy" (Rochester: University of Rochester, Center for the Study of Drug Development, 1977).

R&D investments and the profitability of new products suggested that the return on R&D investment had declined below 5 percent and that the payback period had increased to as much as 19 years.[11] David Schwartzman estimated that the expected rate of return on R&D investment had declined from 11.4 percent in 1960 to 3.3 percent in 1974.[12]

Yet in recent years most major pharmaceutical firms have consistently increased their research spending. Only a small number of firms have either eliminated or sharply curtailed R&D expenditures. One reason for the apparent inconsistency between declining rates of return and increasing R&D budgets is that rising expenditures may mask the fact that firms now undertake fewer projects than they did in earlier years. Because the cost of individual R&D projects has soared in the last decade, firms now tend to select their R&D projects more carefully. Those projects with relatively lower expected returns are less likely to be undertaken. The result is a smaller number of projects, although each is now so much more expensive that total R&D spending is up.

Schwartzman identifies three additional reasons why individual drug firms may maintain their R&D expenditures or increase them, despite a pessimistic overall picture for the industry:

1. Firms may expect to do better than average on the basis of their past records or on the basis of specific research projects already underway.

2. Firms must maintain research staffs and programs if they hope to produce a breakthrough that will inaugurate another stream of innovations.

3. Firms may be willing to gamble in the hopes of beating the high odds against finding a drug that will have sales as huge as those of Valium.

Nevertheless, because of his concern that the deteriorating rates of return will not attract sufficient future investment in pharmaceutical R&D, Schwartzman advocates public policy changes to encourage profit-motivated R&D.

Recent analyses of drug industry profitability have also revealed a discrepancy between real rates of return on R&D investment and published accounting rates of return on stockholder's equity. A significant cause of the apparent inconsistency between the accounting profit rates and the real rates of return on R&D is that companies in their financial reports treat R&D expenditures as a current expense rather than as an investment. Several economists have contended that this inflates the rates of return reported by

[11]Clymer, *loc. cit.*

[12]David Schwartzman, "Pharmaceutical R&D Expenditures and Rates of Return," *Drug Development and Marketing*, ed. Robert B. Helms (Washington, D.C.: American Enterprise Institute for Public Policy Research, 1975), pp. 63–80.

pharmaceutical companies.[13] Thomas Stauffer asserts that these "phantom rates of return" in the pharmaceutical industry obscure a deteriorating profitability picture.[14] Using a sample of six drug companies, another study estimates that capitalization of R&D expenditures would reduce the average rate by 4.4 percentage points.[15] A research report on comparative rates of return for drug and other firms demonstrates that "conventional accounting procedures necessarily result in biased measures of rates of return." Moreover, this bias is not uniform among industries or even different firms within an industry. The study reports that "rates of return that are measured by conventional procedures tend to be most severely overstated in those industries, such as pharmaceuticals, for which research and development constitutes a major proportion of investment outlays."[16]

SOURCES OF PHARMACEUTICAL INNOVATIONS

The origin of pharmaceutical innovations has long been a controversial issue. The debate dates back to the days of the Kefauver committee, which contended that most pharmaceutical discoveries were derived from research work performed outside the industry and the commercial laboratories were primarily involved with molecular manipulations. The industry countered that most of the new drugs that were extensively utilized in 1962 originated in industry laboratories. These opposing views on the sources of significant drug developments have been termed the "battle of the lists."

The controversy relates to three separate, but related, subjects. A first issue deals with the role of the pharmaceutical industry in discovering new drugs. A second question concerns the national origin of new products. Finally, there is the issue of which research approach—molecular modification or theory-based synthesis—has been utilized to discover important new drugs.

[13]Harry Bloch, "True Profitability Measures for Pharmaceutical Investment," *Regulation, Economics, and Pharmaceutical Innovation* ed. Joseph D. Cooper (Washington, D.C.: The American University, 1976); and Robert Ayanian, "The Profit Rates and Economic Performance of Drug Firms," *Drug Development and Marketing*, ed. Robert B. Helms (Washington, D. C.: American Enterprise Institute for Public Policy Research, 1975).

[14]T. R. Stauffer, "Discovery Risk, Profitability Performance and Survival Risk in a Pharmaceutical Firm," *Regulation, Economics, and Pharmaceutical Innovation*, ed. Joseph D. Cooper (Washington, D.C.: The American University, 1976).

[15]J. J. Friedman and Associates, "R&D Intensity in the Pharmaceutical Industry" (Washington, D. C.: J. J. Freedman and Associates, September, 1973).

[16]Baxter & Co., "Comparative Rates of Return for Pharmaceutical and Other Firms: A Conceptual and Empirical Analysis" (Washington, D.C.: Baxter & Co., September, 1974).

Despite the controversy, the available data indicate that pharmaceutical industry sources have discovered most of the new drugs marketed since 1950. Moreover, the relative share of the industry has increased in recent years. Schwartzman estimates that industry sources discovered 86 percent of pharmaceutical innovations between 1950 and 1959 and 91 percent of the innovations during the 1960–69 period.[17]

Similarly, Schnee analyzed a separate sample of new drug introductions and concluded that the share of pharmaceutical innovations contributed by industry sources has risen over time.[18] The proportion of discoveries contributed by drug industry sources between 1950 and 1962 was 62 percent, as compared to 54 percent for the 1935–49 period. An updating of the 1935–62 study indicates that the contribution of nonindustry sources decreased further during the 1960s. Pharmaceutical industry sources originated 89 percent of 87 innovations introduced between 1963 and 1970.[19]

The varying level of participation by countries in the worldwide innovative process affects gaps in technology, shifting patterns of international trade, and the standard of living within a country. Consequently, the role of individual countries in creating and diffusing new technology has become an important public policy issue. The importance of different countries in discovering new drugs was first analyzed in a study by the Organization for Economic Cooperation and Development (OECD) entitled *Gaps in Technology: Pharmaceuticals.*[20]

The OECD studied samples of important new drugs introduced into nine national markets between 1950 and 1967. In seven of the nine countries, the number of important drugs discovered in the United States exceeded the number of drugs from any other single country. For all nine countries combined, the United States, with 67.5 percent, was the most important supplier of important new drugs; Switzerland, with 6.5 percent, was a distant second (Table 3).

In a separate study, using three time periods (1935–49; 1950–62; and 1963–70) Schnee found that the United States consistently accounted for the largest share—approximately 70 percent—in each time period. At the same time, the importance of other countries as sources of innovations has shifted

[17]D. Schwartzman, *The Expected Return from Pharmaceutical Research* (Washington, D.C.: American Enterprise Institute for Public Policy Research, 1975), pp. 9-19.

[18]Jerome Schnee, "Innovation and Discovery in the Ethical Pharmaceutical Industry," in Edwin Mansfield, John Rapoport, Jerome Schnee, Samuel Wagner, and Michael Hamburger, *Research and Innovation in the Modern Corporation* (New York: Norton, 1971), Chapter 8.

[19]Jerome Schnee, "The Changing Pattern of Pharmaceutical Innovation and Discovery," unpublished paper (October, 1974).

[20]Organization for Economic Cooperation and Development, *Gaps in Technology: Pharmaceuticals* (Paris: OECD, 1969).

Table 3. Pharmaceutical Innovations by Country of Origin, 1950-1967

Country	Proportion of Innovations (N = 200)
United States	67.5%
Switzerland	6.5
Germany	5.5
England	4.0
France	3.0
Netherlands	2.5
Denmark	2.0
Other countries	9.0

SOURCE: Organization for Economic Cooperation and Development, *Gaps in Technology: Pharmaceuticals* (Paris: OECD, 1969), p. 127.

markedly over time. Germany, for example, contributed 18 percent of the discoveries during 1935-49 (due to the pre-World War II dominance of the German chemical industry), but only 2 percent of the discoveries during 1950-62, and 7 percent of the discoveries since 1962. In constrast, England's contributions have increased for each time period; it has become the most important foreign source of innovations since 1962, contributing 10 percent (Table 4).[21]

The third and, perhaps, most controversial aspect of pharmaceutical innovation and discovery relates to how new drugs are discovered. The approaches employed to discover drug products are a function of the methods used by pharmaceutical firms to select compounds for biological testing. Pharmaceutical research laboratories utilize one of three methods to choose compounds for biological testing.

First, there is the theory-based approach to synthesizing compounds for biological testing. Under this approach, theories concerning disease processes are used to design a drug to antagonize some biological process in humans. A second approach, termed the random method of selection, is used when neither theoretical considerations nor the activity of previously synthesized compounds provides a rationale for selection of compounds. Compounds are then randomly selected and submitted to high-capacity biological tests in an effort to turn up compounds with the desired activity. The third, and most typical, approach is based on knowledge of structure-activity relationships. Compounds are modeled after an isolated natural product, if one exists, or patterned after structures that may already be known to give the required physiologic response.

It is this third approach which has generated controversy. It has been

[21]Jerome Schnee, "The Changing Pattern of Pharmaceutical Innovation and Discovery," *loc. cit.*

Table 4. Innovations by Country of Origin

Country	Proportion of Innovations		
	1935-49 (N = 25)	1950-62 (N = 43)	1963-70 (N = 87)
United States	70.0%	67.5%	70.6%
England	4.0	9.3	10.0
Germany	18.0	2.3	7.3
France	—	9.3	2.2
Switzerland	4.0	7.0	2.2
Sweden	4.0	2.3	1.1
Other countries	—	2.3	6.6

SOURCE: Jerome Schnee, "The Changing Pattern of Pharmaceutical Innovation and Discovery," unpublished paper (October, 1974).

argued that this emphasis on structure-activity relationships produces research that is inefficient, duplicative, and results in an excessive amount of research effort being devoted to "molecular manipulation." These criticisms are based on serious misconceptions of the nature of the research process and the methods by which scientific advances are made in the life sciences, according to industry scientists. The industry view is that molecular modification is a perfectly legitimate and efficient tool in medicinal chemistry and that its use has often led to the discovery of important new therapeutic compounds. In fact, a study which analyzed the 100 most widely used synthetic or biosynthetic products in 1961 found that 61 percent were analogues or modifications of previously discovered compounds. In other words, structural relationships rather than theoretical drug design considerations were responsible for submission of these 61 compounds to the biological test system which identified their useful properties.[22]

Further evidence regarding the importance of structure-activity relationships is presented in a study conducted by Larry Deutsch. His survey of about 250 physicians to ascertain which drugs they regarded as the most medically beneficial, both generally and in their own practices, indicated that of the 18 drugs most frequently mentioned, 8 resulted from molecular modification. Deutsch concluded that the contribution to improved therapeutics resulting from molecular manipulation, or "inventing around" as he termed it, is substantial. Moreover, these medically significant discoveries would not have taken place under a patent system that offered little or no reward for inventing around.[23]

[22]Maxwell Gordon, "The Business of Molecular Manipulation,"*The Pennsylvania Medical Journal*, Vol. 65 (February, 1962), pp. 191-193.

[23]L. Deutsch, "Research Performance in the Ethical Drug Industry," 17 *Marquette Business Review*, Vol. 17, No. 3 (1973), 129.

REGULATION AND INNOVATION

Throughout this description of the changing pharmaceutical research environment, we have noted the lively controversy regarding the specific role of the FDA amendments in altering the process of pharmaceutical innovation and discovery. While the debate has continued unabated, there were, until recently, no quantitative measurements of the direct regulatory impact. Two pioneering studies have now shed some light on this important topic.

In one provocative analysis, Sam Peltzman concluded that consumers, as a group, incur substantial losses because of the 1962 amendments.[24] Peltzman asserts that the revised regulations have cut the number of new chemical entities introduced annually by half. This has meant net social costs from deaths and illnesses. Moreover, the amendments have served to double the costs of drug development and to reduce competition. The resultant increased drug prices, contends Peltzman, cost the drug consumers millions of dollars more each year.

Peltzman's quantitative estimates of the annual gains and losses are:

1. A loss of $300 to 400 million in missed benefits from the reduced flow of new drugs;
2. A gain of under $100 million from reduced waste on purchases of ineffective drugs;
3. A loss of $50 million from reduced competition from new drugs.

Using these estimates, Peltzman concludes that the measurable effects of the 1962 amendments add up to a net annual loss of $350 million, or about 6 percent of total drug sales.

In a separate study of international differences in the availability, use, and knowledge of new drug products, William Wardell concluded that the post-1962 regulatory environment had produced a "drug lag" in the United States. Wardell examined the pattern of new drug introductions in the United States for the 1962–71 period and compared this pattern with that of England for the same period.[25] Based on a study of 182 new drugs in nine therapeutic areas, Wardell developed the following findings.

First, the number of new drugs which were exclusively available in England (80) was four times the number exclusively available in the United States (20). Second, of the 82 therapies which were mutually available in both countries, 14 were introduced the same year in the U.S. and U.K., 43 were first in-

[24]Sam Peltzman, *Regulation of Pharmaceutical Innovation* (Washington, D.C.: American Enterprise Institute for Public Policy Research, 1974).

[25]William M. Wardell and Louis Lasagna, *Regulation and Drug Development* (Washington, D.C.: American Enterprise Institute for Public Policy Research, 1975), Chapters VI–IX.

troduced into the U.K. with an average lead time of 2.8 years, and 25 were first introduced into the U.S. with an average lead time of 2.4 years. A third Wardell finding was that there were significant differences in the drug lags among different therapeutic categories. The American drug lag was found to be most marked in cardiovascular, gastrointestinal, respiratory, diuretic, and antibacterial therapies.

Finally, Wardell concluded that drugs unavailable in the United States had made a very large impact on the prescribing habits of British medical specialists. The therapy used by these experts was likely to be substantially different from that which could be prescribed by their American counterparts. Most of the American specialists surveyed had a very low level of knowledge about the drugs used by the British experts. Wardell considered the low American awareness of new and, as he noted, even not-so-new drugs both unexpected and surprising.

A recent updating of his original study has convinced Wardell that the gap between the U.S. and the U.K. is closing.[26] Medical practice in the United States is now more in line with therapeutic practices in other developed countries, according to Wardell, who attributes this progress, in part, to a more enlightened regulatory approach in the United States.

SUMMARY

This chapter identified and described seven specific dimensions of the changing research environment of the American ethical pharmaceutical industry and briefly analyzed the economic impact of the altered environment on the technological progress of the industry. First, there has been a sharp decline since the early 1960s in the rate of pharmaceutical innovation. The number of new products reached its peak during the 1951–60 decade. Since then, the annual average rate of new product introductions has declined by one-half.

Second, several theories have been advanced to explain this drop in R&D productivity. Most explanations center on the restrictive impact of the 1962 amendments to the federal Food and Drug Act. An alternative view is that, while we know more about biomedical processes today than ever before, there is a widening biological knowledge gap regarding drug knowledge and disease processes in man.

Third, there have been sharp increases in the cost, duration, and risks of drug development during the last decade. The cost to develop one new pharmaceutical product now approximates $12 million, which is more than ten

[26]*Ibid.*, Chapter X.

times greater than the comparable cost for the pre-1962 period.[27] Similarly, the probability of developing a successful product is close to one-fourth of the pre-1962 success rate.

Fourth, the substantial increases in the cost and length of drug R&D and the accompanying decline in new product introductions have sharply reduced the rate of return on R&D investment. One recent estimate suggests that the expected rate of return on R&D investment dropped from 11.4 percent in 1960 to 3.3 percent in 1974. Despite such pessimistic estimates, most major pharmaceutical firms have consistently increased R&D spending in recent years.

Fifth, pharmaceutical industry research laboratories have discovered the majority of all new drugs marketed since 1950. The industry's role in discovery has increased over time; over 90 percent of the new drugs introduced between 1960 and 1969 were discovered by the pharmaceutical industry. When innovations are analyzed by country of origin, the United States has consistently contributed 70 percent of drug discoveries.

Sixth, consumers, as a group, have incurred substantial economic losses because of the changes in drug laws. The net social costs from the decline in the number of new drugs and the higher prices of existing therapy amount to an annual loss of approximately $350 million.

Seventh, there are substantial international differences in the availability, use, and knowledge of new drug products. When the pattern of new drug introductions in the United States was compared with the pattern in England, a significant American drug lag was found. However, the gap between the two countries has been narrowing.

---

[27]When the cost includes *research* as well and is capitalized, it reaches $55 million per product, according to a University of Rochester study. See Hansen, *loc. cit.*

6

Profitability and the Pharmaceutical Industry

Walter J. Campbell
Walter Campbell Associates

Rodney F. Smith
Assistant Professor
Clark University
Worcester, Massachusetts

INTRODUCTION

Considerable attention has been focused on the pharmaceutical industry's profitability relative to that of other manufacturing industries. There are varying opinions regarding the contributing factors involved. This chapter reviews the concept of profitability. The objective is to provide a framework for logical consideration of the level of pharmaceutical industry profitability.

THE CONCEPT OF PROFITABILITY

Return on Investment

Return on investment is a widely used measure of how well capital suppliers are rewarded for the use of their resources. To calculate return on investment (ROI), a profit figure is divided by the amount of capital invested:

$$ROI = PROFIT/INVESTMENT$$

The resulting ratio can be ambiguous since different commonly used definitions for both profit and investment produce varying measurements for rate of return.* For example, using income before taxes eliminates the effects of

---

*It is not proper to combine just any profit or income figure with just any investment figure. The logic of accounting conventions produces relationships between particular income and investment accounts. Examples of such logical pairings are net operating income with total operating assets and net income after taxes with stockholders' equity.

taxes. Income before financial costs reflects return without the influence of leverage (financial risk). Income after taxes is affected by both tax law and leverage. Other definitions of profit similarly have unique interpretations.

The definition of the capital base is also a source of ambiguity for ROI, since different figures have different interpretations as to the efficiency of an investment. Also, the investment figures are balance sheet items and can be measured at the beginning of the year, end of the year, or the two can be averaged.

Differences in depreciation practice also affect ROI. Assuming the use of net fixed assets, depreciation expense is a current deduction from income, which is offset by an equal reduction in capital invested. As the depreciation schedule is not necessarily the same as the rate of wearing out or obsolescence of assets, depreciation deductions can distort the relation between accounting income and economic rate of return. One study presents evidence that :

> . . . in long-run equilibrium, the forces of competition tend to equalize "cash returns" rather than "accounting returns." The rate-of-return calculation which excludes depreciation deductions approximates the "cash rate of return on gross assets."[1]

The accounting measure, net income after taxes to stockholders' equity (ROE), seems to be the most widely used by government and private analysts in comparing financial performance among and within industries; this measure, however, is subject to significant qualification as the differential impact of inflation, investment in intangible assets, and financial leverage are considered.

Relation to Capital Supply

The total reward flow from an economic undertaking is usually divided into labor, materials and interest expense, and profit, with profit as a balancing item. Profit is a residual and can be positive or negative.

The flow of money capital from surplus spenders (who spend less than their incomes) to deficit spenders (who spend more than their incomes) varies considerably over time in response to political, social, and economic variables, with expected rate of return being particularly important. To induce investment in a given project, capital suppliers require a minimum rate of return which is determined by pure interest plus a premium, usually referred to as a

---

[1]Alexander Barges and Brian R. Hickey, "Drug Industry Profits," *Financial Analysts Journal* (May–June, 1968), p. 80. The profit figure used to calculate economic rate of return would reflect a depreciation deduction just sufficient to replace the capital used up in generating revenue during the profit period.

risk premium, associated with any undesirable investment characteristics inherent in the project. This required rate of return has at least three identifiable levels. The first level is a minimum rate established by administrative costs, time preference, or liquidity preference below which investors will not supply any capital. The second level is determined by opportunity costs, as rational investors will not commit capital to a project that offers a lower return than an alternative project with similar investment characteristics. The third level is the maximum rate obtainable from any project with a given set of investment characteristics.

The first level of required rate of return is established by investors' attitudes regarding capital investment, but the second and third levels are based on individual companies' financial results. Although capital suppliers receive their return as interest, dividends, or capital gains with their preferences determined by the tax structure and brokerage costs, the fact remains that the reward for contributing capital ultimately comes from the profitability of the firm.

Normal Rate of Return

The theory of pure competition includes the proposition that rate of return regulates investment to produce the most efficient allocation of capital. If there is insufficient investment to meet consumer demand, prices are expected to be bid up, which increases return and attracts additional capital. Eventually, according to the theory, prices decline or costs increase until rate of return is again at the normal level with no excess profit.*

Some economists believe the existence of an apparently stable rate above the normal or average can result only from monopolistic behavior.[2] These economists assume that the most likely explanation for relatively high industry rate of return is that existing firms have blocked competitive entry. Therefore, to some economists, stable, above-average rates are proof of a noncompetitive situation. Of course, above-average rates may result from industry structural characteristics without any anticompetitive behavior on the part of existing firms. For example, high capital or technological requirements for efficient production can prohibit competitive entry and result in above-average rates of return.

---

*To the accountant, profit is the revenue remaining after subtracting out costs. To the economist, a normal profit is the reward to the supplier of equity capital and is, therefore, a cost. Return above the normal level is called pure or excess profit.

[2] For an example of this viewpoint, see U.S., Congress, Senate, Subcommittee on Monopoly, *Competitive Problems in the Drug Industry*, statement submitted by Willard F. Mueller (Washington, D. C.: Government Printing Office, 1968), pp., 1806-1861.

The correctness of attributing above-average rates of return to lack of competition can be questioned. For instance, a competitive but high-risk industry might have a higher-than-average rate of return as compensation for above-average risks. A noncompetitive industry might exhibit a below-average return because of continued changes in product demand to which it is expensive and difficult to adapt. This has been explained by Ornstein as follows:

> The pure theory of competition and monopoly does not provide a basis for the traditional hypothesis that with few rivals a firm will earn above average profits. Unanticipated changes in demand and cost or high risk may lead to above average profits in competitive industries and result in differential returns both within and between high and low concentration industries. . . . Hence, above average returns may persist in competitive industries for long periods of time given sufficient disequilibriums, or a monopoly may experience below average profits for long periods depending on demand and cost conditions.[3]

Pure competition is, of course, an extreme or limiting case. One study, relating economic concepts to basic social processes, explains:

> Monopolistic competition can be read simply as impure competition—that is, competition that fails to correspond in every detail with the hypothetical ideal of the theory of pure competition. Thus conceived, it (monopolistic competition) is the competition of any real-world economy.[4]

Social and Political Considerations

It is now part of the political culture to view profitability itself with considerable suspicion. Since the pharmaceutical industry serves people who are ill and sometimes economically disadvantaged, some question whether such an industry should be allowed any profits at all. Thus, because of the nature of the industry's products and because of the lack of public support, suspicion of above-average profitability will likely elicit political pressure, regardless of such matters as risk and uncertainty faced by the industry and the overall quality of its performance.[5]

The first extensive public review of the pharmaceutical industry was initiated in 1959 by the Senate Subcommittee on Antitrust and Monopoly, with

[3]Stanley I. Ornstein, "Concentration and Profits," *Journal of Business* (October, 1973), pp. 519–520.

[4]Robert A. Dahl and Charles E. Lindblom, *Politics, Economics and Welfare* (New York: Harper and Row, 1953), p. 201.

[5]C. Joseph Stetler, President of Pharmaceutical Manufacturers Association, "Are Drug Prices and Profits Without Honor?"; address presented to Pharmaceutical Advertising Club of Newark, May 15, 1975.

Estes Kefauver as chairman. Particular areas of concern were monopoly pricing under patents, lower foreign prices for identical products, identical prices for different companies' products, and promotional activities.

The committee's recommendations were that use of generic name drugs be encouraged, that the existence of side effects be included in advertising, that there be compulsory patent licensing after three years, and that the Food and Drug Administration be given increased regulatory powers. The resulting Kefauver-Harris Act, passed in 1962 after the thalidomide incident, followed some of the committee's proposals, although a compulsory patent licensing provision was not included.[6]

A second major set of hearings by Senator Gaylord Nelson's Subcommittee on Monopoly began in 1967. The main recommendations by witnesses critical of the industry were to encourage the use of generic name drugs and to restrict the patent privilege.[7]

Given the importance of health to society, investigations of the pharmaceutical industry have been complicated by political overtones. An academic researcher generally critical of the drug industry observed that:

> The hearings constitute an interesting and often fascinating contribution to the literature of politics, but are here and there notably incomplete as an exercise in applied economic analysis. In part, this is due to the periodic interference of moral indignation when giving and taking testimony, for the issues investigated were highly controversial. . . . [8]

There appears to be little doubt that public review and scrutiny of the pharmaceutical industry will continue. The set of hearings chaired by Senator Kennedy of the Subcommittee on Health is a significant manisfestation of this process. If the major motivation for political review of the industry is that health care is of the greatest public concern, then it would seem logical and desirable to study extensively the entire system of health care delivery instead of concentrating on only one industry in that system. The Kennedy hearings have, in fact, generally recognized the pharmaceutical industry as an important part but not the only part of the overall health care system that merits intensive review.

---

[6]U.S., Congress, Senate, Subcommittee on Antitrust and Monopoly, *Administered Prices in the Drug Industry* (Washington, D.C.: Government Printing Office, 1960). The following are discussions of the hearings: Richard Harris, *The Real Voice* (New York: Macmillan, 1964) and Estes Kefauver, *In a Few Hands—Monopoly Power in America* (Baltimore: Penguin, 1965).

[7]The hearings are compiled in U.S., Congress, Senate, Subcommittee on Monopoly, *Competitive. Problems in the Drug Industry* (Washington, D. C.: Government Printing Office, 1967-1972). The hearings have yet to be concluded.

[8]Henry B. Steele, "Patent Restriction and Price Competition in the Ethical Drugs Industry," *Journal of Industrial Economics* (July, 1964), p. 198.

VARIABLES ASSOCIATED WITH PROFITABILITY

Market Demand

Much of the attention received by the pharmaceutical industry results from unique consumer demand characteristics. As is illustrated by Table 1, demand for drug products has been growing at compounded rates of 8 percent to 9 percent per year and is expected to continue to do so until 1980. Contributing to this growth will be a slightly older population requiring more medicines, more insurance programs available to more people, continued displacement of hospitalization and surgery (by use of medicines), and generally an expanded capacity for supplying improved health care.

After 1980, drug shipments are expected to grow at a somewhat slower pace, reflecting the expected slower growth in the economy.[9] It would be expected, however, that a given drug will be able to achieve rapid sales growth

Table 1. Federal Reserve Board Production Index for Drugs and Pharmaceuticals

Year	Index
1957	35.9
1958	39.4
1959	44.0
1960	46.2
1961	50.1
1962	56.0
1963	61.8
1964	65.5
1965	75.1
1966	88.7
1967	100.0
1968	111.3
1969	131.2
1970	137.7
1971	157.8
1972	169.0
1973	186.8
1974	193.2
1975	210.6
1980	322.0
1985	440.0

SOURCE: *Predicasts* (April 17, 1975), United States (Financial).

[9] See the "United States Economy in 1985," Bureau of Labor Statistics, 1974, for a discussion of the causes of slower economic growth in the 1980s.

to the extent that it becomes the drug of choice for a particular ailment or that it substitutes for increasingly costly hospitalization or surgery.

A particularly unique characteristic of the pharmaceutical industry may be that product purchase decisions are not much affected by price level. As the individual's health is involved, generally, price is of relatively less importance than quality and availability. Commonly, price is unknown to the consumer at the time the decision to use the product is made.

In a 1971 study which measured the relationship between level of family income and purchase of pharmaceutical products, income was found to have but slight effect on purchase. As shown in Table 2, mean gross drug expenditures per year, during the time period examined in this study (1958-1963), ranged from $30 for families with incomes below $2000 to $52 for those having over $7500. This small range is in contrast to the wider range of $165 to $411 in gross health expenditures per family during this period. In an important study, however, Houthakker and Taylor found that although in the short run drug expenditures are relatively inelastic with respect to total expenditures, in the long run they become very elastic.[10]

Research and Development Activity

Another unique characteristic of the ethical drug industry is its relatively high outlays for research and development (R&D) activity. According to the National Science Foundation figures in Table 3, the pharmaceutical industry allocates R&D expense at the rate of 4.5 to 5.6 percent of sales in contrast to an all-manufacturing average of about 2 percent. The pharmaceutical in-

Table 2. Distribution of Family Drug Expenditures, 1958-1963

Mean Family Income	Mean Gross Personal Health Expenditures per Family	Mean Gross Expenditures for Drugs per Family	Drug Expenditures as Percent of Family Income
All groups	$294	$40	0.75
Under $2000	$165	$30	2.37
$2000-$3499	$226	$35	1.30
$3500-$4999	$287	$40	0.89
$5000-$7499	$336	$41	0.66
$7500 and over	$411	$52	0.50

SOURCE: Hugh D. Walker, *Market Power and Price Levels in the Ethical Drug Industry* (Bloomington, Indiana: Indiana University Press, 1971), p. 11.

[10]H. S. Houthakker and Lester D. Taylor, *Consumer Demand in the United States: Analyses and Projections* (Cambridge: Harvard University Press, 1970), pp. 161-163, 166-167.

Table 3. Industry Research and Development Intensity[a]

Industry	Percent			
	1963	1964	1965	1973
Food and kindred products	b	b	0.4	0.4
Textiles and apparel	0.4	0.4	0.4	0.4
Paper and allied products	0.8	0.8	0.8	0.7
Industrial chemicals	4.1	4.2	3.9	3.0
Petroleum, refining and extracting	1.2	1.0	0.9	0.7
Rubber products	1.6	1.6	1.7	1.6
Stone, clay, and glass products	1.6	1.5	1.5	1.5
Primary metals	0.7	0.7	0.7	0.7
Fabricated metal products	1.4	1.3	1.2	1.1
Machinery	3.1	3.2	3.1	3.2
Electrical equipment	3.6	3.6	3.6	3.6
Transportation equipment	2.5	2.6	2.3	2.9
Aircraft and missiles	2.6	2.5	3.4	2.9
Professional and scientific instruments	4.2	4.2	4.0	4.4
All manufacturing industries — Mean	1.9	2.0	2.0	2.0
Ethical and proprietary drugs	4.5	5.6	5.4	b

[a] R&D expense as a percent of net sales. Company outlays only; government outlays not included.

[b] Not available.

SOURCE: U.S., National Science Foundation, *Research and Development in Industry, 1973* NSF 75-315 (Washington, D. C.: Government Printing Office, 1975), p. 52.

dustry's own calculations show that R&D to sales ratios are much higher: 11.7 percent in 1970, 11.9 percent in 1971, 12.1 percent in 1972, 11.2 percent in 1973, and 11.7 percent in 1974.[11] Research activity seems essential to a pharmaceutical firm's success. Therefore, it is not surprising to find that technological progress is correlated with profit.[12]

PHARMACEUTICAL INDUSTRY PROFITABILITY

Total expenditures on health services and supplies in the United States for 1976 were $139.3 billion. The category of drugs and sundries accounted for $11.2 billion, or 8 percent of the total. This percentage can be compared with

[11]Pharmaceutical Manufacturers Association, *Annual Survey Report: 1974–1975* (Washington, D. C.: PMA, December, 1975).

[12]J. R. Minasian, "The Economics of Research and Development," *The Rate and Direction of Inventive Activity* (Princeton: Princeton University Press, 1962).

the hospital care category at 40 percent of the total, and physicians' services at 19 percent.[13]

Of the total expenditure figure of $11.2 billion, manufacturers of drugs and sundries are expected to receive about 46 percent; wholesalers, 6 percent; and retailers, 48 percent.[14] Since 1958, according to The FTC *Quarterly Financial Reports,* industry profits have averaged 10.2 percent of sales and have ranged between 9.4 percent and 12.2 percent. Applying a range of 10 to 12 percent to the 1976 sales estimate, one arrives at pharmaceutical industry profit estimate of $515 million to $618 million ($11.2 billion × 46% × 10% = $515 million). This equals about one third of 1 percent of the total health care figure of $139.3 billion.

Industry Rate of Return

The basic record of accounting return on equity is set forth in Table 4. Over the 18-year period, 1958-1975, the reported return on equity for all manufacturing companies averaged 11.1 percent and ranged from a low of 8.6 percent in 1958 to a high of 14.9 percent in 1974. For the pharmaceutical industry, average return on equity was 18.1 percent, ranging from a low of 16.7 percent in 1961 to a high of 20.3 percent in 1965 and 1966. Over the entire period, the average pharmaceutical ROI was 63 percent higher than the average ROI for all manufacturing.

Risk and Growth as Determinants of Rates of Return

In a 1967 report, analysts at Arthur D. Little, Inc., measured the spatial variance of returns for companies within some 59 industries and concluded that the spread of returns among companies within a given industry was significantly related to the level of return on total capital.[15]

The authors used risk as a determinant of industry return. Using regression techniques to hold risk constant, they were unable to explain completely drug industry rate of return. Their model predicted a rate of approximately 15 percent, but their observed pharmaceutical industry rate was 17.5 percent, thus leaving an unexplained portion of 2.5 percentage points.

In another study, growth in demand was analyzed as a determinant of drug

---

[13]U.S., Department of HEW, Social Security Administration, "Research and Statistics Note," December 22, 1976.

[14]Pharmaceutical Manufacturers Association, *Fact Book 1976.* (Washington, D.C., PMA).

[15]Gordon R. Conrad and Irving Plotkin, "Risk and Return in American Industry—an Econometric Analysis," (Boston: Arthur D. Little, Inc., 1967).

Table 4. Historical Drug Industry Profitability: Rate of Return on Equity (ROE)

Year	(a) ROE All Manufacturing	(b) ROE Drugs and Medicines	(b) ÷ (a)
1958	8.6%	17.7%	2.1
1959	10.4	17.8	1.7
1960	9.2	16.8	1.8
1961	8.8	16.7	1.9
1962	· 9.8	16.8	1.7
1963	10.3	16.8	1.6
1964	11.6	18.2	1.6
1965	13.0	20.3	1.6
1966	13.5	20.3	1.5
1967	11.7	18.7	1.6
1968	12.1	18.3	1.5
1969	11.5	18.3	1.6
1970	✚ 9.3	17.6	1.9
1971	9.7	17.9	1.8
1972	10.6	18.6	1.8
1973	13.1	19.2	1.5
1974	14.9	18.8	1.3
1975	11.6	17.8	1.5
Low to High	8.65 to 14.9%	16.7 to 20.3%	1.3 to 2.1
Mean	11.1%	18.1%	1.6

SOURCE: Federal Trade Commission, *Quarterly Financial Reports*, various issues.

industry return on investment by Alexander Barges and Brian Hickey.[16] The authors found growth in demand to be a significant determinant. By holding growth in demand constant, Barges and Hickey explained part of the excess of industry return over the all-manufacturing average rate. Their results show a 3.9 percentage point growth premium.

An empirical study by Rodney Smith combines measures of both risk and growth in demand to produce a model with which to study the pharmaceutical industry's rate of return.[17] Using this model, Smith calculated an expected ROE of 18 percent, which was 4.8 percentage points above the observed all-manufacturing rate of 13.2 percent. Presumably, this 4.8 percent reflects a premium for risk and growth in the pharmaceutical industry.

[16]Barges and Hickey, *loc. cit.*

[17]Rodney F. Smith, "Ethical Drug Industry Return on Investment" (unpublished Ph.D. dissertation, University of Massachusetts, 1974).

However, the forecasted rate was still 4.2 percentage points below the observed drug industry rate of 22.2 percent.*

PROFITABILITY AND THE PUBLIC INTEREST

The following list of priorities is offered as a possible description of the public interest as it involves pharmaceutical products:

1. More effective and safe medicines
2. All therapeutic categories fully covered
3. Medicines widely available
4. Reasonable and stable prices
5. Improved medicines for better choice
6. Improved utilization of medicines by physicians and other health care professionals

Of course, most of these are not possible in the long run without financially strong suppliers. Even in an antibusiness environment, there is probably some public appreciation (increased by recent bankruptcies) that financial strength is somehow better than weakness. To depend on unreliable and financially unsure suppliers for vital goods and services is not in the public's best interests. As long as a growing number of improved medicines are provided at reasonable and affordable prices, there is no practical economic reason for consumer agitation simply because pharmaceutical industry ROI is higher than average, especially when profits, as a percent of total health expenditures, are so low and when *manufacturing* profits, as a percent of the consumer's retail prescription dollar, are estimated at less than 5 cents.

Drugs do not comprise a major portion of consumers' budgets and are not principally or even marginally responsible for the rising cost of health care. In fact, drugs generally serve to lower overall health care costs to the extent hospitalization or surgery is made unnecessary. However, drug misuse or overuse may counteract these savings. The public interest requires continued

---

*One reason Smith's 22.2% is higher than the FTC reported rates is because he concentrates on ethical drug earnings, whereas the FTC figures include all "Drugs and Medicines." It should be noted that the investment characteristics included in the Smith model are not measures of market structure. According to the model, a perfectly competitive industry might exhibit an average rate of return above the all-manufacturing average as the result of high variance in returns, positive skewness of returns, and rapid growth. This does not suggest that the ethical drug industry is essentially competitive or essentially monopolistic, only that market structure does not drive the final model and that drug industry ROE can be at least partly explained without reference to posited structural deficiencies in the marketplace.

surveillance to ensure that the cost savings possible are achieved while the wasteful use of drugs is curtailed.

Industry profitability would be constrained:

1. If no new product discoveries of significance are made;
2. If government regulation becomes so expensive that R&D is reduced or eliminated;
3. If patent protection is removed or if patent holders are forced through licensing to give away their exclusive rights to new and successful drugs;
4. If profits or prices are directly regulated.

Given the high value delivered and the low relative cost, most short-term pressures on profits can probably be offset through price increases. However, direct government control of prices will substantially lower profitability over the long term as increases in costs are slow to be offset. The future of the drug industry's profitability may be more a function of political change and public policy than of the underlying economics of supply and demand. To the extent the industry responds effectively to the political process, its profitability may well continue. To the extent political processes are ignored or ineffectively dealt with, the current level of profitability may be unsustainable.

If the future of the industry is to be characterized by artificially low profitability, then it is reasonable to predict a growing inability and unwillingness to reinvest in research and development, fewer innovative advances, and lowering of the quality and availability of medicines originating in the private sector as companies invest their funds in other higher-return opportunities outside of the pharmaceutical industry.

SUMMARY

The rates of return on equity for the pharmaceutical industry have been higher than the overall manufacturing industry average. However, comparing ROEs for different industries without consideration of the determinants of return leads to questionable results. A number of researchers have attempted to empirically verify the relationships between profitability and such variables as risk, growth in demand, R&D intensity, and others. By explicitly considering risk, Conrad and Plotkin, Barges and Hickey, and Smith have been successful in explaining a portion of the difference between the pharmacuetical industry's ROE and the average ROE for all manufacturing industries. Still other investigators have used different models and methodologies to account for the distortions caused by accounting conventions.

There is evidence that the pharmaceutical industry is a target for study because it is highly visible. Yet, the magnitude of industry sales and profits shows that pharmaceuticals comprise a relatively small part of the total health care industry; there is also the possibility that other segments of the health care industry exhibit high rates of return. Because the pharmaceutical industry is comprised of relatively large, national and international firms, their financial data are publicly available. This is in sharp contrast to the situation of individual physicians, private hospitals, some private laboratories, or special facilities such as nursing homes. Due to this lack of relevant data, it is not clear how pharmaceutical manufacturing ROI would compare with the ROI attained in other segments of the health care field. To the extent these other segments produce high-value, relative low-cost products or services, one would expect to find at least the potential for above-average ROI.

7

The Emerging Health Care Environment: Selected Issues

Walter J. Campbell
Walter Campbell Associates

INTRODUCTION

Growth means change. The marked increase in the level of health care services in the United States since World War II has been accompanied by dramatic changes in the way health care is provided, consumed, and regulated. This chapter explores recent changes in the health care environment by considering: (1) the providers of health care (physicians, pharmacists, hospitals, pharmaceutical manufacturers, and other institutions); (2) the consumers (patients); and (3) the regulators (state and Federal legislatures and agencies).

A familiar tale ends with the airplane pilot telling the passengers, "We're lost, but we're making mighty good time." Many observers of the American health care system have concluded that while the system has undergone critical and rapid changes in the last generation, its future direction remains uncertain. As well as discussing where we have been, and why, this chapter discusses where health care in the United States may be going under a national health insurance program.

The author acknowledges the extensive assistance received from Carol M. Cerf of Urban Systems Research and Engineering, Inc., Cambridge, Massachusetts.

1950S AND 1960S: A PERIOD OF DRAMATIC GROWTH IN THE UNITED STATES HEALTH INDUSTRY

All segments of the United States health industry experienced accelerated growth in the 1950s and 1960s. Total national health expenditures climbed from $12 billion in 1950 (4.6 percent of GNP) to $69.2 billion (7.2 percent of GNP) in 1970,[1] rising even faster than the Gross National Product. National expenditures on drugs and sundries grew from $1.6 billion in 1950 (13.3 percent of total) to $7.1 billion in 1970 (10.4 percent of total).[2] In this twenty-year period significant changes occurred regarding recipients, providers, and regulators.

Recipients

The dramatic growth experienced from 1950 and 1960 can partially be attributed to a rising birth rate[3] and growing elderly population.[4] Declines in infant and maternal mortality[5] as well as increased longevity for the elderly population meant more people seeking medical care with drugs, particularly in the case of those 65 years of age and over who constitute about 10 percent of the population, but who are estimated to consume about 25 percent of the drugs.[6]

Increasing affluence and a rising educational level further stimulated the demand for health care. In constant 1958 dollars, per capita disposable personal income rose from $1646 in 1950 to $2610 in 1970, an increase of 59 percent.[7] Better educated people tend to make greater use of health services and are more likely to carry health insurance. Better educated and more affluent citizens are more likely to demand technologically advanced care and higher apparent quality of care. They are more likely to seek preventive care and to be more cautious about taking drugs prescribed by a doctor. However, people with higher incomes generally have fewer health problems than the poor and require less hospitalization.[8]

[1]Nancy Worthington, "National Health Expenditures, 1919-74," *Social Security Bulletin* (February, 1975), p. 9.

[2]*Ibid.*, p. 13.

[3]U.S., Department of Commerce, Bureau of the Census, *Statistical Abstract of the United States, 1974* (Washington, D. C.: U.S. Government Printing Office, 1974), Table 3, Table 9.

[4]*Ibid.*, Table 3.

[5]*Ibid.*, Table 81.

[6]R.A. Ginsburg, *Predicasts Special Report, Drug Industry* (November, 1973), p. 5.

[7]U.S., Department of Commerce, *op. cit.*, Table 186.

[8]Cambridge Research Institute, *Trends Affecting the U.S. Health Care System* (Cambridge, Mass.: Cambridge Research Institute, 1975), pp. 1-12ff.

As income has risen and as the percentage of the population living in poverty has decreased, some of the diseases associated with poverty, malnutrition, and unsanitary living conditions have declined. For example, new tuberculosis cases fell from 76,245 in 1955 to 37,137 in 1970.[9] On the other hand, affluence is creating new health hazards. As Michael Halberstam wrote in the *New York Times,* "our mortality figures reflect convincingly the fact that most Americans die of excess rather than neglect or poverty."[10] One study found that, while more education is associated with relatively low death rates, high income is associated with high mortality when education and medical care are held constant.[11] Thus, the changing character of the population in the United States has altered the character of the demands placed on the health care industry. The demand for tuberculosis drugs has declined as that poverty-associated disease diminishes, while the demand for tranquilizers has soared as more people have become subject to anxiety- related conditions.

Providers

Growth in the Number of Physicians
In the academic year 1950-51, there were 79 medical schools in this country with 26,186 students, of which 6135 graduated that year. In 1970-71, there were 103 medical schools with 40,487 students, of which 10,391 graduated that year.[12] This rapid expansion in medical schools was triggered by substantial government expenditures on research, much of which was done in the medical schools, which helped pay the overhead and salaries at the schools. Beginning in 1963, the federal government also began to make direct grants to medical schools and by 1974, the federal government's role in financing physician education had grown to 60 percent of the total.[13]

Growth in the Number of Hospitals
Between 1950 and 1970 the number of beds in non-federal short-term hospitals rose from 505,000 to 848,000, an increase of 68 percent.[14] This

[9]U.S., Department of Commerce, *op. cit.,* Table 130.

[10]Michael Halberstam, "The MD Should Not Try to Cure Society," *New York Times Magazine* (November 9, 1969).

[11]R. Auster, Il Leveson, and D. Sarachek, "The Production of Health, An Exploratory Study," *Journal of Human Resources*(Fall 1969), p. 430.

[12]Anne Crowley, ed. "Medical Education in the United States 1973-1974,) *Journal of the American Medical Association* (Supplement January, 1975), p. 17.

[13]Dr. Charles Edwards, "The Federal Involvement in Health,"*New England Journal of Medicine* (March 13, 1975), p. 560.

[14]These statistics are for days spent in non-federal, short-term, nonpsychiatric hospitals by the resident civilian population of the United States. American Hospital Association, *Hospital Statistics, 1974 Edition* (Chicago, Ill.: American Hospital Association, 1974), pp. 19-21.

substantial expansion in hospital facilities was stimulated by the Hill-Burton Act, which has provided money for hospital construction since 1946. Specifically, the Hill-Burton program has financed a small but significant portion (15 percent) of annual hospital construction; increased the number of hospital beds, especially in small cities; helped hospitals to modernize; and has been influential in the development of state and regional planning for hospital care.[14a] Medicare-Medicaid and hospital insurance have also helped finance hospital construction since these programs reimbursed hospitals for their depreciation costs. Hospital expansion has been further fostered by hospital insurance, Medicare, and Medicaid which have enabled more people to afford hospital care and have reduced the need for hospitals to provide free care to charity patients.

The Revolution in Medical Technology

National expenditures for health research rose from $110 million in 1950 to $1846 million in 1970.[15] These figures do not include the considerable research outlays made by drug companies, which in 1970 amounted to $559 million.[16] Most of the medical research done outside pharmaceutical firms was financed by the government. The government's share of non-industry funded research continues to rise.[17]

These vast research efforts triggered a revolution in medical technology. New techniques were developed to reduce the incidence of some diseases and shorten recovery time for patients with other maladies. Methods were developed to alleviate or cure health problems that were considered untreatable. However, many whose lives are saved by the new medicines must cope with continuing health problems that necessitate extra medical care for the rest of their lives. In general, not only have the dramatic strides in medical care since World War II increased the demand for health care and for drugs, but the definition of what constitutes "health" was expanded to include the concept of health maintenance as distinguished from health restoration.

The new "medical miracles" resulted in rising expectations: people may tend to expect the medical profession to provide a prompt and complete cure for every complaint; they seek medication to ease every discomfort. The new medical technology has made the health industry more susceptible to

[14a]Judith, R. and Lester B. Lave, "An Evaluation of the Hill-Burton Program, 1948-1973," *The Hospital Construction Act* (Washington, D.C.: American Enterprise Institute for Public Policy Research, May, 1974), p. 2.

[15]Worthingon, *op. cit.*, p. 13.

[16]Pharmaceutical Manufacturers Association, *Fact Book*(Washington, D.C.: PMA, 1973), p. 44. The 1975 figure is probably close to $1 billion.

[17]U. S., Department of Commerce, *op. cit.*, Table 99.

malpractice and damage suits. Thus, in some cases the new technology has raised the level of professional care against which a practitioner's performance will be measured to resolve the issue of malpractice. Some of the new methods have only a small chance of success or may indeed create new medical problems. Some drugs may produce side effects not foreseen when they were introduced. The complex new medical technology has fostered specialization among doctors and other health professionals. Greater efforts now need to be made to keep doctors and other medical personnel conversant with the constant flow of new developments. The new techniques have helped transform our health system into one that emphasizes sophisticated technology and gives a lower priority to simple, basic health care. For instance, large sums are invested in radiation therapy equipment for children who continue to get contagious diseases that could be avoided by relatively inexpensive innoculation programs. Unlike the British health care system, our system tends to emphasize surgery, another expensive procedure, rather than simpler alternatives such as medication.[18]

The high cost of new medical equipment is causing some changes in the structure of our health care system. More doctors are going into group practices. More hospitals are either merging with others or at least sharing some services and/or equipment. Many small hospitals have ceased to exist.[19]

Government

Growth of Health Insurance and Initiation of Medicare/Medicaid

In 1950 only 50 percent of the population was insured for hospital expenses and 36 percent for surgical expenses. By 1970 these figures had risen to 85 percent for hospital insurance and 79 percent for surgical insurance.[20] In 1974, private health insurance was paying 35 percent of the nation's hospital bills and 37 percent of the charge for physicians' services. However, health insurance policies were paying only about 6 percent of the consumer's bills for drugs and sundries.[21]

Following the advent of Medicare and Medicaid in 1965, government programs now pay 53 percent of the nation's hospital bills, 24 percent of charges for physicians' services, and 8 percent for drugs and sundries.[22]

[18]Surgery rates (per 1,000 population) are twice as high in the United States as in England. See: John Bunker, "Surgical Manpower: A Comparison of Operations and Surgeons in the U.S. and in England and Wales," *New England Journal of Medicine* (1970), pp. 135-144.

[19]American Hospital Association, *op. cit.*, pp. 19-21.

[20]Health Insurance Institute, *Source Book of Health Insurance Data 1974-1975* (New York: Health Insurance Institute, 1974), p. 20.

[21]Worthington, *op. cit.*, p. 15.

[22]*Ibid.*, p. 15.

Since consumers now on the average pay 10 percent of hospital bills out of pocket, consumers use and doctors require hospitals stays much more freely. This is one reason that hospital days per 1000 civilian population rose from 900 in 1950 to 1198 in 1970, an increase of 33 percent.[23] Immediately after Medicare went into effect, the use of health services by those 65 and over jumped 25 percent.[24] The elderly, however, are paying somewhat fewer visits to doctors than they did earlier: Medicare and Medicaid have increased access to hospitals more than access to physicians.

Since health insurers in Medicare have generally reimbursed hospitals for their costs, without seriously questioning cost increases, hospital administrators have had no real incentives to keep their costs down — and every incentive to add elaborate new equipment requested by the doctors supplying the hospital with patients. This is one reason why hospital semiprivate room rates rose 380 percent between 1950 and 1970.[25] The galloping inflation in total health care costs has, in turn, stimulated various efforts by health insurers and the government to curb escalation in these costs, as discussed below.

Whether hospital cost inflation can be attributed to "one-shot" developments or can instead be explained by the basic structure of the industry has long been a subject of controversy. A recent analysis commissioned by the Council on Wage and Price Stability concludes that rising hospital costs flow not so much from changing wage rates or other input prices, as from a changing product and increased rate at which the product is consumed.[25a] That is, the problem of hospital-cost inflation is endemic to the structure of the industry and to incentives driving all those involved in hospital care. The Council's overall conclusion, further corroborated by this most recent analysis, is that as presently structured there are few incentives within the provider system to "control costs; to economize, or to weigh the *costs* of a proposed action — the purchase of new equipment, the expansion of a hospital, or the selection of a course of treatment — against its benefits."[25b]

[23]American Hospital Association, *op. cit.*, pp. 19-21.

[24]Jonathan Spivak, "Should Old Folks Pay More for Medicare?" *Wall Street Journal* (March 23, 1973).

[25]"Medical Care: Rising Cost in a Peculiar Marketplace," *Federal Reserve Bank of Richmond Economic Review* (March/April, 1975), p. 11.

[25a]Martin Feldstein and Amy Taylor, *The Rapid Rise of Hospital Costs* (Washington, D.C.: Executive Office of the President, Council on Wage and Price Stability, January, 1977), p. ii.

[25b]*Ibid.*, p. iv.

Pharmaceuticals

With respect to drugs, Congress and the Food and Drug Administration implemented key changes in government regulations. The FDA's primary concern during this period was assuring the safety and effectiveness of marketed drugs, and safeguarding human test subjects participating in clinical drug studies.

Government involvement increased as a result of the thalidomide incident in 1962 when the FDA grew more cautious about approving new drugs. The 1962 amendments to the Food and Drug Act resulted in stricter FDA regulation and enforcement with regard to allowing new drugs on the market, and are substantially responsible for the rapid escalation in the average cost of developing a new drug. The before-tax average investment per new chemical entity is now estimated to be roughly $24 million. In addition, as many as ten years may pass before a drug is marketed and revenues begin to be realized.[26]

Congress also made inquiry into the prices, profits, and economic aspects of the drug industry. The Kefauver hearings beginning in 1959 advanced the thesis that drug prices and profits were too high. Senator Nelson continued the attack in 1967 in hearings before the Senate Monopoly Subcommittee. Most recently, beginning in late 1973, Senator Kennedy's subcommittees on health and on administrative practices and procedures began hearings on the drug industry. These broad-ranging and ongoing hearings (discussed later) have been viewed as critically important to the public, to the industry, and to the FDA.

Along with the FDA's closer scrutiny of drug quality and effectiveness, the Federal government has increased its efforts in the realm of drug abuse with the establishment of the Drug Enforcement Administration and its predecessor agencies.[27]

1970S AND BEYOND: A REVISED GROWTH PATTERN

The health care industry in the United States is no longer growing at the pace that it did in the 1950s and 1960s. Since 1970, health expenditures have fluctuated in growth as a percentage of the nation's Gross National Product. Although total health expenditures rose from $69.2 billion in 1970 to $104.2

---

[26]David Schwartzman, *The Expected Return from Pharmaceutical Research* (American Enterprise Institute, 1975), p. 28.

[27]The Bureau of Drug Abuse Control was established in the early 1960s and was merged in 1968 into the Treasury Department's Bureau of Narcotics to form the BNDD. Congress approved the creation of a new Drug Enforcement Administration (DEA) in 1973 which took over full responsibility for the development of an overall drug enforcement strategy.

billion in 1974, they generally hovered around 7.7 percent of the GNP during those years.[28] In 1975, however, this figure rose to 8.3 percent of the GNP.[29]

Although expenditures on drugs and sundries rose from $7.4 billion in 1970 to $9.7 billion in 1974, a 36 percent increase, roughly one-third of it was simply a reflection of inflation, and the increase was less than the 41 percent rise in drug expenditures during the preceding four years when inflation was less rapid.[30] The expansion of our hospital system has slowed down: while the number of beds in non-federal short-term hospitals grew 9.3 percent between 1964 and 1967, the rate of increase dropped to 7.6 percent during the succeeding three years, and fell still further to 6.5 percent between 1970 and 1973.[31] Although the average daily census in non-federal short-term hospitals grew 11.3 percent between 1964 and 1967, it grew only 8.2 percent during the next years, and a mere 2.9 percent between 1970 and 1973.[32]

There is a variety of factors regarding recipients, providers, and regulators which have resulted in this slowing down of the growth in health care.

Recipients

Lower Rate of Population Growth

Bureau of Census estimates for 1980 indicate that the increase in the American population over 1970 may be as low as 8 percent — in contrast to the 18 percent increase between 1960 and 1970.[33] The birth rate fell from 25.2 per 1000 population in 1957 to 14.9 per 1000 population in 1973.[34] Women today are having only 1.9 children per completed family — less than the current population replacement rate of 2.1 children.[35] Although the fertility rate is falling for women in all socioeconomic classes, the rate is falling faster for low-income women, since family planning services are finally becoming available to them as well as to the middle class, and religion no longer has a

---

[28]Worthington, op. cit., p. 5.

[29]"The Problem of Rising Health Care Costs," Council on Wage and Price Stability (Washington, D.C.: Government Printing Office, April, 1976).

[30]Worthington, op. cit., p. 5.

[31]American Hospital Association, op. cit., pp. 19-21.

[32]Ibid., pp. 19-21.

[33]U.S., Department of Commerce, op. cit., Table 3. This low 1970-80 growth rate would obtain only if the average number of births per 1000 women upon completion of childbearing is as low as 1800.

[34]Ibid., Table 9.

[35]"Birth, Fertility Rates at a New Low in U.S.," New York Times (April 16, 1974), p. 1.

great impact on family planning.[36] While it is always possible that these trends may be reversed, future fertility rates are unlikely to revert to their postwar levels, with effective contraception so widely available.

The impact on health care systems of slower total population growth is being offset, to some extent, by the increasing rate of growth in the elderly sector (age 65 and over). While the total population may grow only 8 percent between 1970 and 1980, the elderly population is expected to increase nearly 20 percent during the decade.[37] Thus, the rapid growth in our Medicare population is increasing the demands on our health care system even as our hospital obstetric units are having a hard time keeping their beds filled.

Growing Public Skepticism about the Health Care Industry

Some of the mysticism that once gave medicine a special aura is fading. An increasingly well-educated population is less awed by the learning of the medical profession and more likely to question doctors' judgments. This is one reason for the rise in malpractice suits in recent years. Health care institutions are also experiencing more public examination and criticism of their operations with growing insistence that the public be given some voice in determining policies. There is a trend toward more citizen participation in the decision processes of health care. Community participation has been written into some federal laws which set up and finance health care programs.

Concurrent with the demand for reasonable, available health care, there has been a growing consumer demand for greater dignity in treatment of the patient. With increasing involvement of community representatives in the planning and management of the health care system, consumer consideration of health benefits has become a standard against which the quality of health care is evaluated. This, in turn, has raised difficult questions about the relationship between medical procedures and actual health benefits, which may in time alter the practice of medicine. Consumer skepticism also works to draw attention to chronic, activity-limiting disease as opposed to the medically more interesting acute maladies, and to the preservation of health as opposed to the care of illness. One of the most persistent critics of the medical establishment, Dr. Sidney Wolfe of the Public Citizens Health Research Group in Washington, predicts that consumer involvement in medical services will lead to the unveiling of such data as death rates in various hospitals, doctors' fees, and professional qualifications.[38]

[36]Edwin Gold, "Public Health Aspects of Future OB-GYN Services,"*Obstetrics and Gynecology* (March, 1973), p. 462.

[37]U.S., Department of Commerce, *op. cit.*, Table 3.

[38]*Business Week* (August 16, 1976), p. 129.

Providers

No profession is immune to the sweeping changes engendered by technologic complexity and the drive toward egalitarianism within society, but the changes within each profession are not the same, and they are being carried out according to different timetables. Physicians are closer to a fundamental restructuring of their traditional ways than many other professions. So massive has been the change in attitudes and procedures that Dr. Theodore Cooper, Assistant Secretary for Health of the Department of Health, Education and Welfare forecasts a "total revision of the (medical) system in the next five years — a reshaping of American medicine."[39]

Over the past decade, physicians have been subject to a host of controls that radically diminished their much-flaunted independence. Established under federal legislation, these controls include health planning agencies (to limit new hospital construction) and physician panels on professional standard review organizations to monitor the performance of other doctors and hospitals (see below). In addition to the widely publicized malpractice suits against individual doctors, recent court rulings that hold hospital trustees personally responsible for malpractice by doctors in their hospitals further intensify the pressure toward greater accountability by the medical profession.

Disenchantment with professionals is largely determined by how frequently and on what terms the public seeks their advice. By this measure, it is understandable why the public is apprehensive about doctors, since probably more people consult physicians than all other professions put together. With the increase in such contacts, the public has taken a less awestruck view of doctors than in the recent past.[40] This may be due in part to the apparent decline in respect for all institutions since the late 1960s, but may also reflect the natural reaction of an increasingly sophisticated public. While the quality of medicine may not have declined, we have a greater awareness of its deficencies, and such factors as rising costs of health care and rising doctors' fees add fuel to the fire.

The idea of reorganizing medical care in a way that will make physicians more responsive to consumer needs is neither new, nor is it as unmindful of technical aspects of medicine as it might at first appear. The informal license that doctors are granted to carry out their work undisturbed results from society's assumption that the result will be for the good of its members. Specifically, it is assumed that there exists in the profession an objective and reliable expertise, so complex that only the properly trained can exercise it.

[39]*Ibid.*, p. 129.
[40]*Ibid.*, p. 129.

Further, it is assumed that this expertise will be faithfully employed for serving the needs of the community, not just of the profession itself or of an elite.

Medical schools and teaching hospitals are providing more training in "family medicine," with practitioners being the modern equivalent of that disappearing breed, the "family doctor" or general practitioner. Simultaneously, efforts are being made to reduce the training program for surgeons and other specialists considered to be abundant in the health care system. If the percentage of specialists among doctors in the United States should eventually shrink, this may reduce hospital utilization. Dr. Cooper of HEW believes that these pressures w ,i lead to new forms of practice. He sees a shift from the current emphasis in institutional care to one favoring more outpatient care and a more realistic approach to preventive medicine.[41]

Health Maintenance Organizations (HMOs)

The last fifteen years has seen a rise in the concept of health maintenance as embodied by health maintenance organizations (HMOs). As presently conceived, an HMO will accept responsibility for the organization, financing, and delivery of health care for a defined population for a fixed, prepaid annual fee. Most HMOs are prepaid groups whose medical professionals work primarily on a salary basis and deliver their services in outpatient facilities or in hospitals owned by the HMO itself. Others are medical foundations, whose doctors treat patients in their private offices and are paid by the HMO on a fee-for-services basis, even though the patients pay for the medical care through a fixed monthly premium paid to the HMO or its insurance carrier.

Some HMOs provide prescription drugs free or at a reduced cost to their members. Other HMOs operate a pharmacy that sells pharmaceuticals at a reduced cost. In such cases, the HMOs encourage the use of generic drugs because of their usually lower costs. Providing care to an enrolled population facilitates the evaluation of performance on the basis of outcomes rather than inputs.[42] If a medical audit reveals no benefits from a drug, its use is curtailed and in this way HMOs are able to evaluate certain drugs.[43] Because HMO doctors, particularly those in prepaid group practices, are subject to close scrutiny by their peers, the doctors are quickly made aware of and heed any HMO determination that a drug is of little or no value.

Statistics on prepaid multispecialty group practices show that the HMO population has improved measures of hospitalization, cost, and mortality as

[41]*Ibid.*, p. 129.

[42]Paul Ellwood, Jr., "The Health Maintenance Organization Approach," *Realigning the Health Care System*, A Report of the 1971 National Forum on Hospital and Health Affairs, p. 21.

[43]Michael Rosenbaum, "HMO: The 'M' Stands for Money,"*Medical Dimensions* (April, 1975), p. 20.

compared to groups under traditional care.[44] Experience in such practices has also shown that planning, budgeting, and management skills can be fruitfully applied to health care delivery. Extensive use of paramedical personnel has also proven effective in HMO-type facilities; indeed, it is through such use that a large part of the cost savings is made.

Historically, the attitude of doctors working in prepaid, comprehensive settings was identical to that of doctors engaged in industrial medicine: concentrate on keeping enrollees off the sick list (as though both the doctor and the patient were employees of the same firm). A negative consideration has been that the patient has little choice in his source of medical care. In recent years, HMO doctors have taken great pride in their position as pioneers and have adopted a proselitizing stance. Membership in HMO-type organizations has been growing steadily as a result of: (1) a deliberate effort to enroll new members; (2) the general dissatisfaction with the fragmented care provided by reimbursement schemes; and (3) the prepaid group's ability to increase their capital investments.

The possibility for increased physician productivity is central to the promise of HMOs in that a partial solution to physician shortages or imbalances may exist. A high physician/population ratio is not directly related to high health outcome (Sweden has about 40 percent fewer doctors per person than the United States; South Dakota has about half the national average of physicians per person, yet white males in that state have the longest life expectancy), [45] but the local supply of doctors has historically been a limiting influence on the effectiveness of medical care.

Use of Paramedical Personnel

It is not possible by 1980 to increase the number of physicians by an amount sufficient to provide 90 percent of Americans with the medical attention now given to the wealthiest 20 percent. The only practical short-term path to expansion of physician care is to increase the utilization of each physician. Paramedical aides and surgeons' assistants are two possibilities for leveraging the physician's time. The number of physician assistants that a doctor can keep occupied varies with the type of practice; for example, pediatricians are likely to be heavier users than are cardiologists. The total number of employees per physician found in multispecialty group practices in the United States has ranged from 3.4 to 5.[46]

[44]Herbert E. Klarman, *The Economics of Health* (New York: Columbia University Press), 1965.

[45]Herbert E. Klarman, "Analysis of the HMO Proposal—Its Assumption, Implications and Prospects," *Proceedings of the 13th Annual Symposium on Hospital Affairs*, Chicago, Ill. (May, 1971), pp. 24–38.

[46]*Ibid.*, p. 24–38.

Curbs Being Imposed on Health Facility Construction

In response to the rapid escalation in health care costs attributed at least in part to the health facility building boom in the 1960s, laws and regulations have been enacted to curb excessive health facility construction by requiring prior approval for capital expenditures. In 1972, the Social Security amendments authorized the government to refuse to include building or depreciation charges in the Medicare-Medicaid payments to any health facilities that ignored a state-designated planning agency's ruling in regard to its capital expenditure plan. In addition, a growing number of states have passed certificate-of-need laws, which require "a determination of need" for capital expenditures and which, in many cases, are more restrictive than the Social Security requirement.

The 1974 National Health Planning Resources and Development Act strengthened these regulations by requiring all states to pass certificate-of-need laws and by expanding the number of health facilities for capital expenditures subject to prior review. Although the widespread adoption of certificate-of-need laws reflects a general belief in the effectiveness of this form of regulation, a number of students of regulation have advanced arguments to the contrary. A recent analysis of the impact of certificate-of-need laws impacts on hospital costs and on the volume of inpatient services concludes that certificate-of-need controls may have in fact contributed to cost inflation, thus producing the very result they were designed to prevent. The study stresses the need for further research concerning the relationship of certificate-of-need controls to other forms of regulation such as rate-setting and PSROs to be discussed later. In addition, the study predicts that the simultaneous application of several types of regulatory controls will become the rule rather than the exception.[46a]

High hospital charges are also being attacked directly by both Blue Cross and government regulators. For most medical insurance plans — including Medicaid and Medicare — doctors and hospital fees are paid on a reimbursement basis, either as "customary" or as a cost-plus plan. Thus, far from being an incentive for economy, such schemes are incentives for maximizing cost; that is, the higher the expenses, the greater the return. Insurers, both public and private, are moving away from such retrospective reimbursements in which health care institutions are reimbursed on the basis of charges or incurred costs and have no incentives to keep their charges or costs low. Instead, insurers are beginning to experiment with prospective reimbursement, which is

---

[46a]David S. Salkever and Thomas W. Bice, *Impact of State Certificate of Need Laws On Health Care Costs and Utilization* (Rockville: U. S. Department of HEW, National Center for Health Services Research, April 17, 1976), p. 3.

based on cost projections and gives providers an incentive to live within their projected budget.

Also, a growing number of states have public rate-setting agencies that establish in advance the rates at which hospitals will be reimbursed with the care provided certain groups of patients (e.g., Medicaid patients and/or Blue Cross patients). The federal government is developing a system to set limits on the rates at which hospitals are reimbursed for the care given Medicare patients. Senator Herman E. Talmadge (D., Ga.) has already proposed a bill that would use federal reimbursements to reward efficient hospitals and penalize inefficient ones.

At present, different limits are set for hospitals of different sizes and in different geographic areas. The National Health Planning Resources and Development Act of 1974 mandates that a more sophisticated rate-setting system be developed that takes into account cost factors beyond the size and location of hospitals. This system may set the stage for federal regulation of all hospital rates if national health insurance is instituted.

Federal efforts to regulate rates are focused on classes and institutions while state rate-setting bodies (and prospective reimbursement schemes by Blue Cross) tend to focus on the projected budgets of individual institutions. These various efforts to regulate hospital rates to date have not been successful in curbing hospital cost inflation, but they have made hospital administrators more cost conscious.

Controls Being Imposed on the Utilization of Health Services

Another cost-control device has been the increasingly determined effort to eliminate unnecessary hospitalization. Health insurers have been under pressure to expand coverage of outpatient care so that patients have no financial incentive to get treatment on an expensive inpatient basis rather than a less costly outpatient basis. Medicare has required hospitals to set up utilization review committees, staffed by doctors, to determine whether patients actually required hospitalization and whether patients were being kept in the hospital longer than was medically necessary.

The Social Security amendments of 1972 created a stronger tool for the control of both costs and quality of care: professional standards review organizations (PSROs), which were to be established in each of 203 areas throughout the country. PSROs are nonprofit associations of physicians, open to and representative of the physicians in the area. However, if the physicians in an area did not create a satisfactory PSRO by January 1, 1978, the Secretary of Health, Education, and Welfare designated some other public or nonprofit organization to serve as the PSRO.[47] PSROs are initially to review

---

[47]Much of this discussion is from Cambridge Research Institute's *Trends Affecting the U.S. Health Care System* (Cambridge, Mass.: Cambridge Research Institute, 1975), pp. III-61ff.

only care provided in health care institutions and will not, at first, review care delivered in a physician's office, clinic, or other ambulatory setting unless the doctors in a PSRO request that it do so.[48]

Unlike utilization review committees, which operate in single hospitals, PSROs monitor the care provided in all institutions in their area. PSROs can accept the review performed by the hospital-based utlization review committees whenever the PSRO determines such review is effective.[49]

PSROs are concerned with more than length of hospital stays. Each PSRO is to draw up standard procedures — or a range of acceptable procedures — to be followed for various diagnoses with various types of patients. It is recognized that there will be instances where a physician's clinical judgment will require him to deviate from the established standards and criteria and, if the judgment is sound, the PSRO will not object to the deviation. If the PSRO should disapprove of a proposed procedure or service or an extension of stay, the government would not pay for the services. However, the physician concerned could appeal the PSRO's determination to the statewide professional standards review council and to HEW. In cases of extreme or repeated violations of PSRO standards, the doctor or provider can be fined up to $5000.[50]

The standards and criteria established by each PSRO are to reflect acceptable patterns of practice in the PSRO's area and will take into account the professional personnel, facilities, and equipment available in the area. PSRO guidelines are expected to be modified periodically as experience is gained and as new developments occur.[51] However, restricted by PSRO guidelines, doctors will find it difficult to experiment with new techniques or procedures. On the other hand, publication of the norms of diagnosis and treatment can alert physicians to alternate or newer methods of care. PSROs could eventually be used to assist the FDA and the drug industry in analyzing the efficacy of drugs, both to identify those that are ineffective and to identify unexpected benefits and/or undesirable side effects.

PSROs will compile up-to-date profiles on individual physicians to spot doctors who overprescribe certain drugs, overutilize certain procedures, or otherwise fail to meet stipulated guidelines.[52] In two existing review organizations, a physican advisor reviews all requests for admissions or extensions made by a limited number of practitioners put on "full review" because of many suspect or questionable admissions or billings. The names of the doctors

[48]*Ibid.*, pp. III-61ff.

[49]*Ibid.*, pp. III-61ff.

[50]*Ibid.*, pp. III-61ff.

[51]*Ibid.*, pp. III-61ff.

[52]"PSRO: A Report," *Health Care Today* (January—February, 1974), p. 3.

on full review are kept from the public, but the doctors themselves are told when and why they are listed.[53]

Although the doctors are moving reluctantly to establish PSROs the government is determined to establish some sort of review of medical care and will eventually find some means of doing so with or without the doctors cooperation. This will inevitably introduce more caution into medical practice: hospital stays, diagnostic tests, surgery, and drugs will be prescribed less freely than at present.

Utilization review committees have already reduced the average length of stay in non-federal, short-term hospitals from 8.4 days in 1968 to 7.8 days in 1973 and have played a role in slowing the rise in hospital admissions.[54]

Drug Equivalency
The issue of drug equivalency is having an impact upon drug pricing. Many chemically equivalent drugs are sold at widely varying prices, and if these drugs are deemed therapeutically equivalent (on the basis of such parameters as bioavailability and quality assurance data), the health care professional deciding which drug is to be prescribed or dispensed may be sufficiently concerned with price to select the lowest-priced "equivalent" drug. Several segments of the industry and the public have assumed that equivalancy will mean significant cost savings in the use of lower-priced generic drug products. As the practice of medicine has become more institutionalized, purchasing agents for large hospitals, buying groups, HMOs, and some large retail pharmacy chains—all of whom play an influential role in the selection of drug therapy—will increase the pressures to substitute "equivalent products" where cost savings are possible.

Although drugs still must be prescribed by physicians, the choice of which particular drugs will be inventoried by the institution is frequently determined by a cost-conscious administrator. Also, there is a growing attitude among certain segments of the trade that the physician's authority to determine choice of drug therapy should be balanced with pricing and cost issues.

If a national health insurance system were adopted which required the dispensing of lower-priced generic drugs, the impact on the drug industry would be significant—particularly under a system that covered drugs taken outside the hospital. Approximately 60 percent of the 200 most prescribed drugs are presently available in generic form.[55] (Generically written prescrip-

[53]"Peer Review Now: PSRO at Work," *Modern Health Care* (January, 1975), p. 51.

[54]American Hospital Association, *op. cit.*, pp. 19-21.

[55]John P. Curran, "Multi-Source Drugs: An Acceleration in the Use of Lower Costing Substitutes?," Reynolds Securities Information Report, May 13, 1977.

tions account for 10 percent of all prescriptions.[56]) Even without national health insurance, the use of generic drugs is likely to grow as consumers become more sophisticated about drug pricing and as concern about costs grows among doctors, particularly those practicing in HMOs. Drug companies heavily dependent on branded drugs with generic competitors may thus encounter some drop in profitability, because prices may be forced down, even if sales continue to rise. This could result in these companies reducing certain capital or long-term expenditures such as new product research. Many manufacturers already have launched price-competitive generic products in recent years — reflecting an appreciation for growing third-party pressures to hold drug costs down.

Regulators

Food and Drug Administration

There are a number of environmental factors that have been influential in bringing about changes in FDA drug policy over the last decade. As noted earlier, during the 1950s and 1960s the FDA's primary concerns were assuring the safety and later the effectiveness of drug products. The FDA has now, however, become increasingly concerned with the prices of prescription drugs and possible barriers to competition.

This new concern of the FDA has been illustrated in the agency's regulation of "new drugs." The FDA seems to be returning to the concept that some human prescription drugs will be considered by the agency to be "not new drugs" and hence marketable by any person as long as certain minimum standards are met. The minimum standards might be set forth in a monograph for a drug or drug class, or might simply be those standards, such as regulations governing current good manufacturing practice for finished pharmaceuticals, applicable to all drug products. Eliminating "new drug" requirements would more easily enable new competitors to enter the market. While the FDA cannot implement this policy with impunity (as was demonstrated in a federal court decision[57] requiring the FDA to properly enforce the "new drug" provisions of its operating statute), the agency nevertheless seems to be moving in the direction of attempting to foster greater competition in the industry.

It is no surprise that in the current environment the FDA has increased its attention to economic issues of health care. After many years of Congressional complaints that the drug industry's prices and profits are excessive, public belief in the validity of the charges has increased. Also, Medicare and

[56]*Ibid.*

[57]Hoffmann-La Roche Inc. v. Weinberger, et al, (Memorandum Opinion), Federal District Court, District of Columbia, July 19, 1975.

Medicaid have become realities, and a national health insurance system is anticipated.

Additionally, FDA has been forced to reexamine the nation's basic drug regulatory structure as Congress moves toward what is likely to be the most comprehensive reform of drug laws since 1962. As the Agency promotes its own views, individual legislators have proposed major amendments of their own. Congressman Paul Rogers (D.-Fla.), Senator Edward Kennedy (D.-Mass.), and Senators Jacob Javits (R.-N.Y.) and Harrison Williams (D.-N.J.) have introduced important proposals relating to such matters as conditional new drug approval, patient package labeling, and patent law reform.

Federal Trade Commission

The FTC is examining the structure of the pharmaceutical manufacturing industry. Specifically, the FTC is concerned with the drug industry's high return on equity (reportedly 18.8 percent in 1974 versus 14.9 percent for all manufacturing) and is questioning whether the drug industry is in some fashion illegally restraining trade or engaging in monopolistic activity. A recently approved study has been undertaken by the FTC to investigate the marketing of multisource drugs and the effects of state antisubstitution laws. The purpose of this investigation is to determine whether consumers are subject to unfair or deceptive acts or practices in connection with the sale of multisource prescription drugs.

It is also known that the FTC will examine certain therapeutic markets, such as the cephalosporins, to see if anticompetitive practices exist therein.

Maximum Allowable Cost Program

With respect to cost controls on the use of pharmaceuticals, hospitals and other institutions providing care to Medicare and Medicaid patients are now required to use the lowest cost drugs which are widely and consistently available, as detailed in HEW's maximum allowable cost (MAC) regulations.[58] This means that, in many cases, hospitals will use generic drugs rather than brand-name drugs. A generic drug is one which is sold under a common, established, nonproprietary name no matter which company manufactures it, and which has an unpatented active substance. A brand name is used by a manufacturer to distinguish its drug from those manufactured or sold by others. Most if not all patented products bear brand names. Generic drugs are often priced less than brand-name drugs and their use for Medicare and Medicaid patients, according to some sources, could save the government $60

---

[58]U.S., Department of HEW Press Release, January 20, 1975, quoted in *Medical Care Review*, February 1975, p. 118.

to $75 million a year.[59] Drug companies, while acknowledging the usually greater profit on branded drugs, have argued that a brand-name drug may be of higher quality or effectiveness than its generic equivalent and that substitution of generics for the prescribed branded drug without the physician's consent interferes with the practice of medicine.

State Drug Substitution Legislation

Most states still retain laws prohibiting pharmacists from dispensing a drug other than that specifically prescribed by the physician. However, a growing number of states (currently about twenty) now permit the pharmacist to substitute a chemically equivalent drug for the prescribed drug. This development has found a solid base of support in some pharmacists' associations and in state and national consumer groups, such as public interest research groups and the American Association of Retired Persons. Indeed, federal legislation repealing state prohibitions against substitution is being considered. Whether or not allowing substitution actually generates consumer cost savings will remain uncertain until more experience is gained.

Central Procurement

The concept of central procurement is particularly applicable to generically equivalent drugs available from several sources, since the government can purchase the drug on the basis of competitive bidding among the various manufacturers who enter the bidding process.

Central procurement is not new; the federal government, through its Defense Procurement Supply Center (DPSC) and other purchasing units, has used it for years. Most recently, however, the state of California has embarked on a new application of central procurement of prescription drugs for use in its Medi-Cal (Medicaid) program. Under the California scheme, the state would purchase and take title to drugs and arrange for their distribution to wholesalers who, in turn, would distribute them to pharmacists. The pharmacists would dispense the drugs to patients for use in the state program. Both wholesalers and pharmacists would receive a service fee from the state and would have no investment in the drugs.

Central procurement has never been applied to a Medicaid system in this manner, and its result is uncertain. California intends to implement the concept on a pilot-project basis for test purposes before undertaking it on a full scale. Pharmaceutical manufacturers, drug wholesalers, pharmacists, and physicians have voiced several reservations to California's implementation of the concept. They question its cost effectiveness, its potential adverse impact

---

[59]"Drug Industry Fails to Block U.S. Price Plan," *Wall Street Journal* (July 28, 1975), p. 3.

on the quality of drug care, its uncertain impact on the efficiency of the drug distribution process, and its potentially negative impact on the future of the various segments of the industry. In view of the considerable controversy generated by central procurement, its use in Medicaid programs (or in a national health insurance program) is not certain, although the biases of cost consciousness argue for it.

A POSSIBLE FUTURE: NATIONAL HEALTH INSURANCE

Although numerous developments in the 1970s have served to slow the growth of the health industry, before the end of the decade a new program may be instituted by the new Carter administration which may retrigger the previous pattern: national health insurance.

National health insurance is being advocated for three reasons: (1) many of the poor and near poor have no health insurance, and Medicaid coverage is inadequate and varies greatly from state to state; (2) those who do have health insurance often have insufficient protection for catastrophic illnesses; and (3) current health insurance pushes the system into emphasizing high-cost care, discourages preventive medicine, and does nothing to promote efficiency.[60]

National health insurance proposals take a number of forms. The most limited proposal is that of Senators Russell Long (D., La.) and Abraham Ribicoff (D., Conn.).[61] Their proposal would leave existing private insurance intact, but would create two new federally administered programs: catastrophic illness insurance, which would provide protection for everyone covered by Social Security and which would be administered by the Security Administration; and a federal medical insurance assistance plan, providing protection for the poor and medically indigent, and replacing Medicaid.

At the other extreme is the Kennedy-Corman[62] plan, which would provide comprehensive coverage for the entire population with eventual coverage for dental care. Also, many other legislative plans include some coverage for general preventive health care, particularly for children. Most of the other proposals would provide comprehensive health insurance protection for all residents of the United States, although different insurance plans would cover different segments of the population. In general, the proposals would provide one plan for the employee (paid for by joint employer-employee contribu-

---

[60]Cambridge Research Institute, *op. cit.*, pp. III-61ff.

[61]H.R. 10028 and S. 2470, Catastrophic Health Insurance and Medical Assistance Act, 94th Congress, 1st Session (1976).

[62]H.R. 21 and S. 3, The Health Security Act of 1975, 94th Congress, 1st Session (1976).

tions) and separate plans for the aged (an improved Medicare) and for the poor and medically indigent (replacing Medicaid).

The Kennedy plan[63] (supported by labor), the Ullman plan[64] (supported by the AMA), and the McIntyre plan[65] (supported by the health insurance industry) all provide significant coverage for prescription drugs. In addition, all plans specify a deductible (a certain sum to be paid on health care bills before health insurance coverage goes into effect) and have coinsurance provisions (a certain percentage of health care bills to be paid by the beneficiary even when the care is covered). A major difference between the various proposals is the portion of national health expenditures that would be financed publicly. Those proposals providing for financing by payroll taxes rather than by premiums would make national health insurance appear more expensive because all the cost would show up in the federal budget.

The inevitable impact of any national health insurance program would be increased national health expenditures directly proportional to the extent of the coverage. The range would be from $3.4 billion, under the Long-Ribicoff bill, to $13 billion under the Kennedy-Corman bill.[66] Personal health expenditures in 1975 totaled about $103.2 billion. Thus national health insurance would raise these expenditures 3.3 percent to 12.6 percent.[67] A Rand study estimates that national health insurance will also increase the demand for hospital care by about 5 percent to 15 percent—an increase with which the existing hospital system can cope without undue strain.[68]

Regarding ambulatory physician services, where the financial barriers to care are higher than for hospital care, national health insurance might increase the demand by 30 percent to 75 percent, depending upon the deductibles and coinsurance provisions.[69] Such a jump in the demand for physicians' services is likely to seriously strain our health care system. As a result, physicians' fees would probably rise rapidly, patients would experience long waiting time for appointments, and/or physicians would be able to give less time to each patient. In addition, there may be a spurt in the sales of prescrip-

---

[63]*Ibid.*

[64]H.R. 1 and S. 2470, The National Health Care Services Reorganization and Financing Act of 1975, 94th Congress, 1st Session (1976).

[65]H.R. 5990 and S. 1438, The National Health Care Act of 1975, 94th Congress, 1st Session (1976).

[66]U.S., Department of HEW, *Estimated Expenditures under Selected National Health Insurance Bills, A Report to Congress,* July 1974.

[67]*Ibid.*

[68]Joseph Newhouse, Charles Phelps, William Schwartz, *Policy Options and the Impact of National Health Insurance* (Santa Monica: Rand Corporation, June 1974).

[69]*Ibid.*

tion drugs, as more people have access to a doctor who can prescribe drugs for them.

CONCLUSION

The emerging health care environment will be characterized by (1) higher levels of health care delivery to more people; (2) higher levels of public review, regulation, and control; and (3) higher levels of capacity utilization, especially for the individual physician but probably also for the hospitals, pharmacies, and health product manufacturers.

The conflict of public policy objectives and ultimate taxpayer costs will not go away; indeed, balancing improved levels of delivery and increased costs is likely to become more difficult as medical science adds new and even more expensive, but life-saving, procedures and apparatus and as the entire production and delivery process comes under ever-increasing scrutiny.

National health care insurance will be the most important new development in the health care environment, affecting providers, recipients, and regulators in different but significant ways. Providers of health care will be forced to produce more of it; regulators will have a much larger job controlling what transpires; and recipients will have fewer choices but will, on average, enjoy a greater level of service. Implementation of national health insurance will be considered effective public policy to the extent it can (1) provide the public with equal access to quality health care; (2) distribute the costs of services equitably; and (3) avoid overburdening the existing health care structure or unfairly burdening the average taxpayer.

Conclusion

Cotton M. Lindsay
Associate Professor
Department of Economics
University of California, Los Angeles

Two concerns generate much of the governmental and popular interest in the pharmaceutical industry. First, there is concern that the prices paid for drugs are excessive, that is, higher than is "reasonable." Second, there is concern that drugs be both useful and safe. Drug purchasers quite naturally seek help from drugs — not additional sickness or suffering. Before we can adequately assess government intervention to promote any of these objectives, however, we must understand those peculiarities of the pharmaceutical industry which validate these concerns.

Profits and prices of food and clothing are topics of considerable concern to most households; these items are as important to life and health as are the products of pharmaceutical companies. Yet the principal thrust of government policy in both of these areas has been to keep prices up rather than to lower them.* It would take us far beyond the scope of this chapter to explain this unusual practice with respect to these two industries, but certain peculiarities are present in the market for pharmaceuticals which differentiate it from most industries serving the American household. Taken together, these suggest that the forces of competition and consumer scrutiny, conventionally relied upon for these results, may not be sufficient to produce here either adequately low prices or reasonably safe and efficacious products.

First, consumers (that is, patients) have inadequate knowledge of the therapeutic and other properties of drugs to make reasonable judgments in the market about their purchase. They must rely on the advice of their physi-

---

[1]Agricultural price support programs and commodity import quotas have significantly raised prices in this country, while tariffs and import quotas on foreign textiles have had a similar effect on the prices of clothing. D. Gale Johnson, *Farm Commodity Programs: An Opportunity for Change* (Washington, D.C.: American Enterprise Institute for Public Policy Research, 1973).

141

cians and their pharmacists for this information, neither of whom bears the direct economic cost of such decisions. Such a situation may lead to weakened price sensitivity on the demand side of the market for pharmaceuticals. In the absence of strict legal accountability on the part of these professionals, it might also lead to inadequate concern for the safety and efficacy of preparations prescribed.

Second, the medical profession itself depends to a significant degree on pharmaceutical companies for information concerning marketed drugs. As most of this information is transmitted predominantly in terms of brand names, further market power may be conceded to the sellers of pharmaceuticals. Moreover, marketing costs may appear wasteful because they seem to be principally directed toward capturing a larger market share and thus seem self-defeating from the point of view of the industry as a whole. If all sellers reduced their investments in marketing, these lower costs might be passed on to consumers in the form of lower prices.

Finally, new pharmaceuticals are protected by patents granted by the federal government. A patent is in effect a government protected monopoly over the sale of the patented product. Regardless of the essential competitiveness of the industry, the price charged by a company for a patented drug is shielded from cheaper copies of other sellers. Until that patent protection expires or more effective substitutes are introduced, the price will be the monopoly price. It will exceed the marginal cost of producing the drug.

All of these features combined have led to a number of laws, regulations, and proposals for new laws and regulations whose consequences occupy much of the discussion in the papers in this volume. First, the consumers' informational plight in this market has seemed to justify intervention to protect them from two threats: excessive market power of drug suppliers and potentially harmful chemicals whose properties they cannot be expected to understand. Second, this same informational difficulty is alleged to produce the wasteful competitive marketing expenditures which make operations more costly than they need otherwise be. Finally, patents themselves, by virtue of the monopoly power they confer, may result in prices and profits that would not exist in an economic system which does not provide incentives for innovation.

Ultimately, however, policy must be considered in terms of its predicted results—not in terms of the desirability of the phenomenon with which it is intended to deal. It is therefore vital that the consequences of policies considered to deal with the peculiarities of this industry be well understood. It is quite plausible, for example, that prescribing physicians are less sensitive to cost than consumers would be if they could themselves choose among available drugs—that is, if the consumers had access to and could evaluate the same information that physicians have. To the extent this is true, the market falls short of this benchmark of abstract perfection, and some government intervention may therefore be warranted. Such interventions do not, however, invariably produce perfection themselves.

The available options for dealing with this problem all must be directed toward preventing manufacturers from taking excessive advantage of whatever market power such arrangements confer. These may be achieved by profit or price controls, directly or indirectly, via such schemes as mandatory cross-licensing of patented drugs, requiring prescriptions by generic rather than drug brand name, or shortening the period of patent protection. Each of these would clearly result in lower profits for drug companies and might result in the lowering of some drug prices. Other predicted consequences of such actions raise serious reservations about their use, however. Thus, it is of some importance to develop analytically the full range of results of these policies — both positive and negative.

PROFIT AND PRICE REGULATION

First, let us consider the consequences of profit or price controls. Profit controls or "rate of return regulation" is widely practiced for public utilities, and its results have been widely and carefully studied. This approach seeks to keep prices low by tying price increases to the profitability of these firms. If the rate of return falls below what is considered acceptable, the regulated firm may be allowed to increase its prices. Excessive profits, on the other hand, result in a lowering of prices and even rebates to past customers.

While this approach may seem quite reasonable, economists are far from a consensus on the desirability of rate of return regulation, even for public utilities. The adverse results identified for this approach in that application are even more troublesome for an industry as complex as pharmaceuticals. As Averch and Johnson (1962)[2] have pointed out, rate of return regulation causes firms to adopt inefficient production techniques involving excessive use of capital. Second, as Alchian and Kessel (1962)[3] demonstrate, the attenuated property rights of owners of such enterprises lead to a slackening of cost-consciousness. There is little incentive for managers to be vigilant to possible ways to cut costs if such cost reductions are accompanied by wholly offsetting reductions in revenues through price cuts.

Most important, however, is the effect such regulation is predicted to have on research and development within these firms. High-risk investment must

[2]H. Averch and L.L. Johnson, "Behavior of the Firm Under Regulatory Constraint," *American Economic Review*, Vol. 52 (December, 1962), pp. 1052–1069.

[3]Armen A. Alchian and Rueben A. Kessel, "Competition, Monopoly and the Pursuit of Pecuniary Gain," *Aspects of Labor Economics* (Princeton: National Bureau of Economic Research, 1962).

pay high rates of return in order for it to be attractive to those bearing the risk. Little risk is associated with investment in public utilities. Demand is stable, and, until recently when fuel prices became highly variable, costs were reasonably predictable. By contrast, the research and development engaged in by pharmaceutical firms is precisely the sort of risky investment that requires high yields. A firm may risk high odds to develop a drug if it stands to earn a sufficient profit on a successful product. Controls that inhibit the ability of firms to recoup the costs of these research programs also inhibit the willingness of firms to engage in the development of new products. Economic analysis suggests that any lowering of the profits of pharmaceuticals through regulation will ultimately be translated into a reduction in the rate at which new drugs will be introduced. The desirability of regulation of profits must therefore be gauged by comparing the predicted price reductions with some evaluation of the "drug lag" caused by this regulation.

Price regulation is similar in most effects to profit regulation. Direct price controls can quite obviously keep the money price of drugs down. Unless some attention is paid by regulators to the effects of such controls on profits, however, serious results may arise in markets for both new and existing drugs. If, for example, prices are held so low that rewards to producing and marketing them are seriously eroded, then such controls may affect the availability of drugs. For this reason, enlightened price control tends to be identical with profit control, and poorly managed price control tends to be worse. Again, therefore, we see that the value of any obtainable reduction in price must be offset against the deterrent effect on development which is implicit in these controls.

OTHER CONTROLS ON MARKET POWER

Alternative methods of addressing the market advantage which pharmaceutical suppliers wield over consumers are shortening or eliminating the period of protection for patented drugs, mandatory cross-licensure of patented drugs, and enforced substitution of lowest-priced generic equivalents for brand-identified prescriptions. Each of these should have the effect of lowering prices of some drugs.

By shortening or eliminating the patent protection which producers of covered drugs now enjoy, governments effectively reduce the monopoly power of the producers. Other suppliers may engage in the manufacture and distribution of these products without the threat of prosecution for patent infringement; hence, the prices of these products may be driven downward. Mandatory cross-licensure — the granting of manufacturing rights to competing firms with little or no compensation to the patent holder — has the same effect. As the drugs involved have already been developed, this policy obviously has no effect on their availability. As far as these drugs are concerned, reducing the patent protection of their developers effectively reduces the prices and the profits of the patent owner.

Such policies can be counted upon to affect the availability of yet undiscovered drugs, however. The length and extent of protection of their patent rights are of direct importance to pharmaceutical firms contemplating their commitment to research and development. If these firms perceive that such protection is likely to be attenuated in the future, they will undoubtedly translate this into diminished profitability, hence diminished economic attractiveness of investment in the development of new products. These policies can be expected to reduce the extent of investment in research and development by pharmaceutical firms and thus to reduce the rate of introduction of new vaccines and medicines.

This is not to say, of course, that such a policy is necessarily undesirable or unwise. Prices of certain drugs will undoubtedly fall in the short term, and such reductions may outweigh the cost of the lag imposed in the introduction of new drugs on the market. In other words, quite conceivably there may be excessive investment in drug research and development, with the result that new discoveries are being introduced more rapidly than is warranted by economic efficiency. This issue cannot be resolved here, nor is it likely that an exclusively economic answer exists to this question. If it is decided that excessive resources are being devoted to research, shortening the patent period will correct this. As weakening of the patent rights of drug developers will have an undeniable effect on the rate of discovery and introduction of new drugs, the desirability of adopting this policy on other grounds should therefore be weighed in terms of this predicted result.

GENERIC AND BRAND-NAME DRUG PRESCRIBING

Patent protection is not the only feature of the market for pharmaceuticals which gives producers power over their prices. Physicians rely on the marketing messages of pharmaceutical firms for information on new drug developments, and this information is transmitted understandably in terms of these firms' chosen brand names for the products rather than their generic names. This brand-name association may lead to prescription of brand-name drugs in preference to chemically equivalent and sometimes cheaper substitutes, even when there are no demonstrable differences in the effectiveness or quality of the alternative products.

Recognition of this problem has led to a number of suggestions, several of which have been implemented on a limited scale. One is to allow (or require) pharmacists to substitute cheaper, chemically equivalent generic drugs for drugs which are prescribed by brand name. Of these two, the former seems particularly attractive, since it suggests a valid function for the skilled pharmacist whose role since World War II has almost vanished in the supply chain of pharmaceutical products from producer to consumer.

These proposals have not been universally acclaimed, however. Some physicians have objected to both practices on the ground that they interfere with the independence of physicians in doing what they believe is best for patients. This argument appears to have validity, for individual patient's responses to different but chemically equivalent drugs may indeed differ. In such circumstances, a physician may have good reasons for prescribing by manufacturer rather than by chemical identity.

There are two less obvious problems with these policies which must also be given consideration. The first of these concerns a connection once again between the activity and the profitability of new drug development. It is not merely the continuing visits of detailmen nor the advertising in professional publications which leads to the brand-name identification of chemical products. The lengthy period when the producer has patent protection (and thus is the only source of a product) itself results in some association of the drug with the original producer. This identification may persist after the patent has lapsed. The attachment is itself a source of continuing profits to producers and thus is a part of the "life cycle" of anticipated economic rewards to new drug development.

Policies that result in the substitution of competing drugs for higher-priced branded drugs will reduce the profits earned during the post-patent protection period of each drug's "life cycle." Expected profits associated with the development of any new drug will thus be adversely affected by such a policy, leading to diminished investment in development. Again, therefore, the short-run advantages of the policies in reducing the costs of drugs currently on the market must be considered against the adverse effect of the delay imposed on the introduction of new and vital products.

Another important effect of substitution of generic for brand-name drugs is that such a policy would dramatically alter the attractiveness of investment in marketing. As Harrell pointed out in Chapter 4, virtually the entire marketing budgets of pharmaceutical firms currently are directed at the prescribing physician. A significant part of this expenditure finances the corps of "detailmen" who personally call upon physicians to present the marketing messages of the manufacturers whom they represent. This focus on the physician is quite understandable in view of the pivotal role which he currently plays in the purchase decision. If that role is altered by legislation that effectively eliminates the physician's right to select the source of the drugs he prescribes, this will obviously affect the attractiveness of investment in influencing his prescription decisions. Firms will devote fewer resources to this sort of marketing, and to the extent that pharmacists will be constrained to deliver the lowest cost product, competition will be limited to price, and expenditure on marketing, in general, will decline.

To the extent that such expenditure is wasteful, this result is, of course, to be applauded. That is, if the resources devoted to marketing serve no useful economic function except to attempt to attract buyers away from rival firms, then a policy which has the effect of discouraging this use of resources is desirable. It is far from clear, however, that marketing expenditures are completely wasteful in this sense. Research cited in Chapter 4 suggests that marketing information provided by producers through detailmen and printed advertisements is an important source of data on new drugs and pharmaceutical products for physicians. It is reported, furthermore, that physicians tend to place considerable credence in this information. This latter result may be reinforced by FDA monitoring of such information to insure its factual content.

A policy that discourages investment in marketing of products may, therefore, weaken the informational network on which physicians rely for news of product developments in the pharmaceutical industry. We may deplore this dependence on nonprofessional sources of such information, but it is far easier to decry this situation than to design an alternative system of getting the information to physicians. Pharmaceutical companies now have a considerable stake in developing and improving this network, and its importance to physicians is itself valid proof that it has been and is effective.

By removing an individual physician's power to select the manufacturer of the drugs he prescribes, the incentive of manufacturers to supply physicians with this information is reduced. We may be sure that under these circumstances fewer resources will be devoted by them to this activity. Other channels may, of course, be developed. We must not take for granted, however, either their emergence or their effectiveness in transmitting this information. Substitution of generic equivalent drugs for brand-name products may sometimes result in lower prices to consumers for some drugs. The advantages of such price reductions must, however, be weighed against both the retarding effect of this policy on the development of new drugs and its effect on the flow of information concerning these discoveries from their developers to physicians.

In summary then, attempting to lower prices through regulation or reduction in the market power of pharmaceutical firms does not seem to offer very promising prospects. The scope for reducing prices by squeezing profits seems quite negligible on the one hand, and the penalties in terms of delays are potentially quite significant. These statistics cannot provide the final answer to issues of the importance of those raised here. Considerable disagreement exists over the actual responsiveness of new drug development to changes in the profitability of research. Sources of the divergence of pharmaceutical rates of return from the average of all manufacturing industries continue to be explored. On the other hand, precipitous new legislation in this area may ultimately do more harm than good.

The miracle of twentieth-century medicine has been in large part the miracle of chemical agents and vaccines. This century has witnessed the defeat of one killing or debilitating disease after another by the introduction of sulfonamides, antibiotics, and vaccines. Chapter 3 chronicled the dominant role played by pharmaceutical and chemical companies in the development of these drugs. This country has a considerable stake in the vigor and economic health of its pharmaceutical industry. We cannot afford to take lightly either the life-saving legacy we owe it or the future miracles it may hold for us.

INDEX

Abbott, 29, 66, 77
Acenocoumarol, 56
Acetanilid, 24
Acetophenetidin, 24
Acetylsalicylic acid, 16
Advertising, 82-83, 85-86, 147
    impact, 73-75
Affluence, health care and, 120-121
Allergy specialists, 71
Allopurinol, 64
American Home Products, 25, 29, 77
American Medical Association, drug ratings,
    15, 44-45, 46, 49
Aminopterin, 59
Amyl nitrite, 24
Anesthesiology specialists, 71
Angina pectoris, 55
Animal tests, 16-17
Anisindione, 56
Anorexics, 31
Anthelmintics, 31
Antianxiety drugs, 49, 50
Antiarthritics, 63, 64, 67
Antibacterial drugs, U. S. lag, 103
Antibiotics, 42, 45-46, 67, 95
    heart diseases, 54-55
    mortality decline, 44
    new firms, 31
Anticoagulants, 54, 56
Anticonvulsants, 31, 66
Antidepressants, 49
Antihistamines, 42, 49, 95
Antihypertensives, 31, 42, 54, 67
Anti-infectives, sales, 27, 78
Antiinflammatory agents, 64
Antipyrene, 24
Antispasmodics, 95
Arrhythmias, 55

Arteriosclerosis, 53, 54, 55, 56, 57
Arthritis, 62-64
Aspirin, 24
Asta-Werke, 60, 62
Ataractics, see Tranquilizers
Athrombin-K, 56

Barbiturate, 24
Biologicals, sales, 27, 78
Blood lipid level, 42
Blood pressure, 54
Blue Cross, 131, 132
Brand-name drugs, 87, 145-147
Breast cancer, 59, 61-62
Bristol-Myers, 25, 29, 77
Bronchial dilators, 31
Brookhaven National Laboratories, 65
Burchenal, J. H., 60
Burroughs-Wellcome, 29, 60, 64, 77

Cancer, 58-62, 67, 95. See also
    Neoplasm drugs
Capital supply, 106
Carbamazepine, 66
Carbidopa, 65
Cardiovascular disease, 27, 53-58, 78
    specialists, 71
Carter-Wallace, 92
Celontin, 66
Central nervous system drugs, sales, 27, 78
Cephalosporins, 136
Cerebrovascular diseases, mortality, 55, 57
Chemneo, 74
Children's Cancer Research Foundation, 59
Chloral, 24
Chloramphenicol, 46
Chlorazepam, 66
Chlordiazepoxide, 50, 51

Chloroform, 24
Chlorothiazide, 54
Chlorpromazine, 49-50, 51
Chlortetracycline, 46
Cholesterol levels, 42, 54
Ciba-Geigy, 29, 66, 77
Civil War, drug industry, 23-24
Clinical testing, 16-18, 19
Clonopin, 66
Colon cancer, 59, 62
Competition, 27-29, 107-108
Compound E, 63
Congressional inquiries, 10, 11, 108-109,
    125, 136
Construction, curbs on, 131-132
Consumerism, health care, 127
Contraceptives, 25, 31, 42
Coronary heart disease, 53
Coronary vasodilators, 31
Corticoids (corticosteroids), 42, 63-64, 67, 95
Cortisone, 63
Cotzias, George, 65
Coumadin, 56
Cumopyran, 56
Cyclocumarol, 56
Cyclophosphamide, 60, 62
Cytosine arabinoside, 60

Death rates, U. S., 43-44, 48, 53-55, 56, 57,
    59, 67
Denmark, innovation source, 100
Dentists, distribution channel, 88
Depo-Provera, 19
Dermatologicals, 27, 78
Dermatology specialists, 71
Detailmen, see Salesmen
Dexamethasone, 63
Diabetic drugs, oral, 42
Diagnostic agents, 27, 78
Diazepam, 50, 51
Dicumarol, 56
Digestives, sales, 27, 78
Dilantin, 66
Dipaxin, 56
Diphenadione, 56
Diphenylhydantoin, 66
Diphtheria, death rates, 48
Direct mail advertising, 73, 83, 85
Discoveries, see Innovations
Distribution, 88-89
Diuretics, 31, 42, 54, 103

Diversity, market share and, 76, 77
Dopamine, 65
Drug Evaluations, 15
Dysentery, mortality, 44, 48

Ear-nose-throat specialists, 71
Educational level, health care and, 120-121
Efficacy, drug, 10, 11, 12, 13, 16
    foreign data, 19-20
    market mechanisms and, 141, 142
Emergency medicine specialists, 71
Endo, 56
Endocardium, chronic disease of, mortality,
    56, 57
Endocrine drugs, sales, 27, 78
England, innovation source, 100, 101
Epilepsy, 65-66
Equivalency, 3-4, 134-135, 145-146
    state legislation, 137
Ether, 24
Ethosuximide, 66
Ethrane, 19
Ethyl biscoumacetate, 56
Excess profit, 107-108

Farber, Sidney, 59, 60
Federal Trade Commission, 136
Fleming, Alexander, 45
5-Fluorouracil, 62
Folic acid, 59
Food and Drug Administration (FDA), 3-4,
    10-20, 70, 82-83, 85, 86, 135-136
    costs to consumer, 102-103, 104
    innovation, 76, 78-79, 102-103, 125
    reorganization, 136
Food, Drug, and Cosmetic Act, 9, 10
    1962 amendments, 3, 10-14, 76
    proposed amendments, 19
France, innovation source, 100, 101

Gastroenterology specialists, 71
Gastrointestinal drugs, U. S. lag, 103
Geigy, 56
General practice specialists, 71
Generic drugs, 14, 15, 82
    Medicare/Medicaid, 136-137
    prices, 87, 144, 145-147
    see also Equivalency
Genitourinary system drugs, sales, 27, 78
German measles (rubella), 44, 47, 48
Germany, 24

innovation source, 100, 101
Gout, 42
Gouty arthritis, 63
Government purchases, central
    procurement, 137-138
Gross National Product, 26

Health care, national expenditures, 120,
    125-126
    providers, 121-122, 128-130
    recipients, 120-121, 126-127
Health insurance, 123-124, 138-140
Health maintenance organizations, 129-130
Health services utilization, 132-134
Heart disease, death rates, 56, 57. See also
    Cardiovascular disease
Hedulin, 56
Hench, Philip S., 63
Heparin, 24, 56
Heparin sodium, 56
Hill-Burton Act, 122
Hodgkin's disease, 61
Hoffman-La Roche, market share, 29, 77
    products, 51, 56, 61, 62, 92
    research, 46, 50, 65
Hormones, steroid, 63
Hospitals, charges, 123-124, 131-132
    drug distribution, 88-89
    expansion, 121-122
    utilization, 132, 133, 134
House Health Subcommittee, 136
Hydrocortisone, 63
Hypertension, 55, 56, 57
Hypertensive heart disease, 53
Hypnotics, 31

ICI, 66
I. G. Farbenindustrie, 45
Incidence data, diseases, 47-48, 67
Income levels, drug expenditures, 111
Indomethacin, 64
Infectious diseases, 44-49
Inflation, health care costs, 36, 124
Influenza, mortality, 44, 48
    vaccines, 47
Information sources, drugs, 15, 73-74, 75, 147
Innovations, 11, 24
    categories, 43, 76-79, 93, 95
    costs, 96-98, 103-104
    national origins, 43, 99-100, 101
    profitability, 92

regulations, 6, 76, 78-79, 102-103,
    144, 147-148
research methodology, 98, 100-101
    see also Research and development
Insulin, 24
Internal medicine specialists, 71
International Drug Monitoring Program, 18
Ischemic heart disease, mortality trends, 57
Isoniazid, 46

Javits, Senator Jacob, 19
Johnson & Johnson, 25, 29, 77
Journals, professional, 83, 85-86

Kefauver-Harris Act, 6, 109
Kefauver hearings, 10, 11, 108-109, 125
Kendall, Edward C., 63
Kennedy, Senator Edward M., 19, 20, 109,
    125, 136

Labeling, 82-83
L-dopa (levodopa), 19, 65
Lederle Laboratories, market share, 29, 77
    R and D, 46-47, 59, 60, 62
Lee, Philip (HEW), 42, 66
Leeds University, 61
Leukemia, 59-61
Levodopa, 19, 65
Librium, 92
Life expectancy trends, 43-44
Lilly and Company, 23-24
    market share, 29, 77
    products, 60, 61
Liquamar, 56
Lung cancer, 59

McNeil Laboratories, 25
Macrolides, 46
Malaria, 44
Malpractice and damage suits, 123, 127, 128
Manufacturers, 26-30, 40
    new firms, 25, 31
Marketing, 69
    costs, 79-83
    targets, 70-72
    trends, 77-78, 89-90
Market mechanisms, 141-143
Market research, 72, 74
Market share, 30. See also specific
    manufacturers
Mayo Clinic, 63

Mead Johnson, 62
Measles (rubeola), 42, 44, 47, 48
Mechlorethamine, 61
Medi-Cal, central drug procurement, 137-138
Medical education, 129
Medical Letter, The, 15
Medical technology, 122-123
Medicare/Medicaid, 123-124
　hospital construction, 131-132
　maximum allowable cost program,
　　136-137
　utilization review, 132-134
Meningitis, 44
Meningococcal infections, 48
Mental health facilities, 50, 51, 52
Mental illness, 49-53
Mephenytoin, 66
Mercaptopurine, 60
Merck & Company, 25
　market share, 29, 77
　R and D, 45, 64, 65
Merck Sharp & Dohme, 54
Mesantoin, 66
Metabolic drugs, sales, 27
Methadone, 19
Methotrexate, 59, 60, 62
Methsuximide, 66
Milontin, 66
Miltown, 92
Miradon, 56
Monopoly, 107, 108, 136
　Congressional hearings, 10-11,
　　108-109, 125
MOPP program, 61
Mortality data, *see* Death rates
Mumps, 42, 44, 47, 48
Myocardial insufficiency, 56, 57
Mysoline, 66

National Cancer Institute, 61
National health, 44
National health insurance, 138-140
National Health Planning Resources and
　Development Act, 131, 132
Nelson, Senator Gaylord, 109, 125
Neoplasm drugs, sales, 27, 78
Netherlands, innovation source, 100
Neurology specialists, 71
New products, *see* Innovations
Nitroglycerine, 24
Nitrous oxide, 24

Oberval (France), 56
Obstetrics and gynecology specialists, 71
Occupational medicine specialists, 71
Oncovin, 61
Ophthalmology specialists, 71
Oral cancer, 59
Oral contraceptives, 25, 31, 42
Oral diabetic drugs, 42
Oral diuretics, 42
Organon, 56
Ortho Pharmaceutical Corporation, 25
Osteoarthritis, 63
Oxytocics, 31

Package insert, regulations, 15
Pancreas, cancer of, 62
Paradione, 66
Paramedical personnel, 130
Paramethadione, 66
Parke-Davis, 23
　market share, 29, 77
　R and D, 46, 66
Parkinsonism, 64-65
Patents, 142, 143, 144-145. *See also*
　Brand-name drugs
Pathology specialists, 71
Pediatrics specialists, 71
Penicillin, 24, 31, 45
　synthetic, 46, 67
Pfizer, 25, 29, 77
Pharmacists, 73, 88-89
Phenacemide, 66
Phenindione, 56
Phenoprocoumon, 56
Phensuximide, 66
Phenurone, 66
Phenylbutazone, 16
Physicians, information on drugs, 73-74, 75
　marketing target, 70-72
　numbers, 71, 121, 130
　professional review of, 132-134
　public attitudes to, 127, 128
Physician-patient relationship, 13-14
Physicians' Desk Reference, 73
Pills, Profits and Politics, 42, 66
Pneumonia, 44, 48
Poliomyelitis: incidence, 47, 48
　mortality, 44
　vaccines, 42, 46-47
Polymixins, 46
Population growth, 127-128

Postmarketing surveillance, 17-18, 19, 20
Preclinical (animal) tests, 16-17
Prednisone, 60, 61, 63
Premarketing clinical trials, 17-18
Prescribing practices, 72-75
  U.K., 103
Prices, flexibility, 35
  market mechanisms, 141-143
  regulation, 143-145, 147-148
Pricing, 33-34, 35, 36, 37, 40, 86-87, 134-135
Prinidone, 66
Probenecid, 64
Procarbazine, 61
Procurement, central, 137-138
Products categories, sales, 27, 78
Product decisions, 75-79
Production, growth of, 110
Professional standards review organizations, 132-134
Profitability, 34, 36, 37, 38-39, 40, 112-115, 116, 117
  capital supply and, 106-107
  competition and, 107-108
  demand and, 110-111
  innovation and, 92
  measures, 105-106, 116
  social aspects, 108-109, 115-116
Profit regulation, 143-144, 147-148
Promotion, costs, 69-70, 79-86
  restraints, 81-83
  targets, 70-75
Prontosil, 45
Proprietary drug companies, 25
Prostate, cancer of, 59
Psychiatry specialists, 71
Psychostimulants, 31
Psychotherapeutic drugs, innovation trends, 95
Public Citizens Health Research Group, 127
Public health, 44, 130
Public interest, profitability and, 115
Pulmonary disease specialists, 71
Pure Food and Drugs Act (1906), 9

Radiation, leukemia, 60
Radiology specialists, 71
R and D, see Research and devlopment
Rectum cancer, 59, 62
Regulation, governmental, 9-21, 82, 136-138, 144, 147-148
Research and development (R and D), 25,

30-33, 67, 91-92, 103-104
  costs, 40, 96-98, 103-104
  expenditures, 58, 92, 112, 122
  see also Innovations
Respiratory system drugs, 27, 78, 103
Retailers, distribution by, 88-89
Rheumatic fever and heart disease, 53, 55, 56, 57
Rheumatoid arthritis, 63
Rhone-Poulenc Company, 49, 51
Rickettsia organisms, broad-spectrum antibiotics, 46
Risk, economic, 115
Robins, 29, 77
Roche, 66
Rocky Mountain spotted fever, 46
Rogers, Representative Paul, 136
Rubella, 44, 47, 48
Rubeola (measles), 42, 44, 47, 48
Rutgers University, 45

Sabin, Albert, 46
Safety, 16, 74, 141-143
  postmarketing surveillance, 17-18, 19, 20
Sales, leading firms, 27-30
  product categories, 27, 78
Salesmen, cost of, 83-84
  functions, 73, 74, 84-85
  technical expertise, 84-85, 89, 90
Salk, Jonas, 46
Salvarsan, 24
Samples, 86
Sandoz, 51, 66
Sandoz-Wander, 29, 77
Schering, 56, 60, 61
Schering-Plough, 29, 77
Searle, 29, 77
Sedatives, 31
Senate Subcommittee on Antitrust and Monopoly, 10, 11, 108-109, 125
Senate Subcommittee on Health, 20, 109, 125, 136
Senate Subcommittee on Monopoly, 109, 125
Sharp and Dohme, 23, 64
Silverman, Milton, 42, 66
Sintrom, 56
Skin cancer, 59
Sloan-Kettering Institute, 60
Smallpox, 44
Smith Kline & French, 29, 51, 77
Specialists, 71, 129

Squibb & Sons, 23, 29, 77
Sterling, 29, 77
Sternbach, Leo H., 50
Steroid hormones, 63
Stomach cancer, 62
Streptomycin, 45
Stroke, 53
Sulfa drugs, *see* Sulfonamides
Sulfanilamide, 9, 10, 24
Sulfonamides (sulfa drugs), 31, 42, 44-45, 67
Surgery, specialists in, 71
Surveillance, postmarketing, 17-18, 19, 20
Sweden, innovation source, 101
Switzerland, innovation source, 99, 100, 101
Syphilis, 44

Talmadge, Senator Herman E., 132
Technology, 122-123
Tegretol, 66
Testing, 4, 10, 11, 12, 15-18, 19, 20
Tetracyclines, 46
Thalidomide, 11
Thioguanine, 60
Thioridazine, 51
Thyroid preparations, 31
Tranquilizers (ataractics), 31, 42, 49-53, 92
Triamcinolone, 63
Trichomonacides, 31
Tridione, 66
Trifluoperazine, 51
Trimethadione, 66
Tromexan, 56
Tuberculosis, 44, 46, 48
Typhoid fever, 44, 48
Typhus, 46

United Kingdom, new drug availability, 103
United States, innovation source, 99, 100,

101, 103
Public Health Service, 47
regulations, *see* Food and Drug
    Administration
Senate hearings, *see* Senate Subcommittee
    on Antitrust and Monopoly; Senate
    Subcommittee on Health; *and* Senate
    Subcommittee on Monopoly
Upjohn, market share, 29, 77
    R and D, 56, 60
Urology, 71
Uterus, cancer of, 59

Vaccines, 42, 44, 46-47, 67
Valium, 92
Vasoconstrictors, 54, 67
Vasodilators, 54, 67
Vincristine, 60
Vitamins and nutrients, 27, 42, 78

Waksman, Selman, 45
Walker, 56
War, drug industry and, 23-24, 25
Warfarin potassium, 56
Warfarin sodium, 56
Warner-Lambert, 29, 77
Wellcome Research Laboratories, 60
Wholesalers, distribution by, 88, 89
Whooping cough, 44, 47, 48
Wisconsin, University of, 56, 62
Wisconsin Alumni Foundation, 56
Wolfe, Sidney, 127
Wonder drugs, 24
World Health Organization, 18
Wyeth Company, 23

Zarontin, 66